The
War That Saved
the Whales

The Confederate War Against
the Yankee Whalers

By

Captain Paul Watson

I looked into the eye of a dying whale and there I saw pity, not for himself or his kind, but for us, that we could kill so ruthlessly, so thoughtlessly, so mercilessly, and for what?

For our sins Leviathan dies, and when the last whale is slain, humanity will itself fall victim to our own ecological insanity, for the fate of the whale is our fate, for when the whale is gone, the oceans will die and when the oceans die, we die!

—Captain Paul Watson

Published by Focsle LLP, Annapolis, Maryland

Copyright © 2019

ISBN: 978-0-9600391-0-4 (Hardcover)
ISBN: 978-0-9600391-2-8 (eBook)

Table of Contents

Foreword

In his work *The History of the Peloponnesian War*, Thucydides writes that there are three reasons for conflict or war: honor, fear, and national interest. The last reason has included a variety of causes such as territorial expansion, the domination of trade, colonization, and security of resources. Resources drive economies, enable trade, satisfy a hungry nation, provide energy, and employ citizens. European empires fought each other hundreds of years ago over the control of Indonesian spices, such as nutmeg in the Banda Islands. In the twentieth century, access to oil was one of the many reasons that helped fuel – literally and figuratively – the Second World War including the embargo of oil exports to the growing Japanese empire. One can read Pulitzer Prize — winning author Jared Diamond's *Collapse: How Societies Choose to Fail or Succeed* to get a sense of the impact of the ecology and the failure of critical resource management. In the twenty-first century, we can expect further conflicts to arise over diminishing resources, particularly those that are essential to survival. One of those will undoubtedly be the impact of marine life.

Study after study predicts the collapse of most sea life by mid-century from overfishing and illegal fishing. Competition for fish as a staple for human or animal consumption will only grow. This has already occurred in southeast Asia and incidents off South America where territorial nations have fired on Chinese fishing vessels, suggesting the possibility of other regions where conflict might erupt. Studying wars and conflicts over these resources can be useful.

This work by Paul Watson is important for three reasons. First, it is an important but little-told part of American Civil War history.

Second, it is a cautionary tale of the impact of whaling. Third, Watson proves how understanding military history can be applied to modern issues and maritime operations.

The American Civil War has always been a popular subject for historians and those interested in reading history. It was the culmination of a nearly century-old ideological battle over the federal system, the role of the national and state governments, and how it manifested itself through the issue of slavery. America's Civil War battlefields are still highly visited today. Given that so many American lives were lost during the Civil War than were lost by the U.S. compared to all other wars in which it was involved, it is understandable that army battles, operations, and generals have received most of the attention.

The Navy – both Union and Confederate – played important roles to differing degrees. Historians have begun addressing this gap in military history such as Bill Fowler's *Under Two Flags*, Craig Symonds' *The Civil War at Sea*, Jamie Malinowski's *Commander Will Cushing: Daredevil Hero of the Civil War* and books about the exploits of individual ships like the Confederate raiders. This book by Watson takes on the mission of several raiders by attacking the Union through its economy, specifically the whaling industry.

By the Civil War, whaling had a long history going back prior to the Revolution when more than 350 whalers put to sea. Whales were seen as a commodity. Nothing more, nothing less. Perhaps it made it easier to hunt them when they were deemed monsters of the deep. While we could look at how whales were viewed starting with the Old Testament story of Jonah being swallowed by a whale, American literature was filled with man's fight with whales. Nathaniel Philbrick recounts the story of the Nantucket whaleship *Essex* in the southern Pacific after being attacked by a whale. The story was well known by the U.S. Navy which had recently stationed ships off the west coast of South America to protect whaling ships from pirate attacks or other threats. A formal Pacific Squadron was established in 1821 with the ship-of-the-line USS *Franklin* and schooner USS *Dolphin* in the decade that the United States would overtake England in the whaling industry.

Newspaper editor Jeremiah Reynolds would write an essay titled *Mocha Dick* for the Knickerbocker Magazine. It was one of the influences of Herman Melville's seminal work, *Moby Dick*. Reynolds likely had another motive for his essay as he was one of the proponents of a South Seas Exploring Expedition to survey islands to assist and expand American commerce, including whaling, in the Pacific, eventually established in 1838 with six ships and under the command of Lieutenant Charles Wilkes. To support this mission, the Navy intended to enlist experienced deckhands from the whaling centers of New Bedford and Nantucket.

The Navy nearly got into a conflict in the 1830s over access to marine resources in the Falkland Islands. The Connecticut-based *Harriet*, under Captain Gilbert Davison, had arrived in the Falklands in November 1830 for sealing and whaling. He was warned by a local administrator not to take any seals in his jurisdiction. Doubtful of the man's authority since American ships had operated in the region for a century and there were questionable claims on the area, the *Harriet* continued its work and returned in 1831. It and several other American ships were captured nearly leading to a conflict over this local resource.

America supplanted England as the largest whaling nation in the 1830s. In 1828, the gross tonnage of all American merchant ships engaged in whaling was 54,000 gross tons (whalers were generally a few hundred tons.) By 1837, that had increased to 129,000 gross tons. It would finally peak in 1857 when the total gross tonnage was 195,000.

Maritime destiny was the belief that America's future lay on the oceans, not merely in its lands. The term, which first appeared in *Miriam Coffin, or the Whale Fisherman* by Joseph Hart (1834), predates the stated concept of Manifest Destiny by more than a decade. That it initially appeared in a work of fiction should not diminish its importance or value. On the contrary, its advent suggests the fundamental nature of maritime destiny and popular support. Hart's story focused on the Nantucket whaling industry, an enterprise that had been under the Navy's protection.

Hunting whales was acceptable for two reasons. First, their oil was an important resource. Second, the whaling industry's ability to slaughter and harvest whales depended on the concept that they weren't sentient, and they were fundamentally dangerous to humanity, even though whales never acted in concert to destroy man. A war on whales was easy as a result. Human history is replete with wars that have been justified by portraying the enemy as less moral, less intelligent, less human. During the American Revolution, British cartoons showed John Paul Jones as a black-bearded pirate with a skull-and-crossbones on a bicorn. During heated negotiations between the Americans and French at the outset of the Quasi-War, the XYZ affair had cartoons showing three well-dressed, distinguished American diplomats on the one side and a multi-headed French revolutionary negotiating as a guillotine does its work in the background and citizens eat rats at a "civic feast." American papers portrayed the Spanish Empire as a giant ape brutalizing the people of Cuba. This is part of how wars are conveyed and even campaigns between political ideologies. Each side tries to assume the moral ground, giving each side the necessary reason to conduct war or a political campaign. Therefore, wholesale slaughter of whales was deemed accepted as they were not considered sentient. Nor was their role in the global maritime ecosystem considered.

This book is also important in how prior military operations can be applied to current or future operations. Like many Americans, I was introduced to Sea Shepherd through its cable television series *Whale Wars*. As someone who had served at sea in the navy, my strong critique and initial skepticism on the tactics employed slowly shifted to curiosity and then to objective analysis. I then interviewed members of Sea Shepherd as I prepared for teaching a class in modern maritime security. I first met Paul Watson at his home in Vermont in 2016 to interview him for a four-part series on marine resources and Sea Shepherd that appeared in the online version of *The National Interest*. My intent was to learn more about overfishing and how Sea Shepherd developed. While in his office I was immediately struck, however, by the history books and ship models. We quickly started discussing the Civil War and the impact of the Confederate raiders on Union whaling. At that point, I knew there was something different about Sea Shepherd's fleet, operations, and tactics. It had a founder and leader who not only had a clear mission but used history to help guide him. As he writes in these pages, "It has always been my understanding that history is most useful as a guide for actions in the present. We learn from the mistakes and the successes of the past. In order to fight whalers in my lifetime, I needed to know how others fought whalers in the past...I employed their logs to locate whaling grounds and I tailored some of their tactics to stop the whalers."

Attacking whaling was important in several wars. U.S. Navy Captain David Porter in command of USS *Essex* during the War of 1812, sailed for the south Pacific, specifically to the Galapagos, to attack British whaling, disrupt their commerce, and draw British warships away from the Atlantic area of operations. If this sounds familiar to some, it was the premise for the Patrick O'Brian-based movie *Master and Commander* starring Russell Crowe. In the movie, Crowe's British warship chases a French frigate on its way to disrupt British whaling activity in the Pacific, particularly the Galapagos. When shipping insurance rose due to wartime or pirate activity, policy-makers take heed. It was as true during the American Revolution and War of 1812 as it was a decade ago when Somali pirates attacked and held for millions of dollars of ransom supertankers and freighters. In terms of the Civil War and the subject of this book, Watson rightfully points out that "Dabney wasn't saving whales. He was hitting the Union at its economic heart."

What I brought back with me from my first meeting with Watson wasn't only content for a series of articles for *The National Interest*, it was a direct application for the students whom I teach in naval history. Every day I try to find one lesson from the past and compare it to some contemporary naval or maritime issue. When I now teach the naval portion of the Civil War, I include the example of Paul Watson and Sea Shepherd comparing what they do with the Confederate raiders.

Sea Shepherd's mission is one that in actuality transcends both nation-states and political ideologies. Overfishing, illegal fishing and depletion affect all of us whether in terms of short-term economics or long-term basic survival in the delicate balance of our global eco-system. The tactics they and Paul Watson have used to that end are discussed in this book.

And so begins the tale...

Claude Berube, PhD

HUNTING WHALERS

Introduction

The modern-day movement to defend and protect the world's whales has an unusually, close connection with the American Civil War.

Since 1975, I have led the international high seas movement to save the whales on the high seas, commanding dozens of ships intervening against numerous whaling operations around the globe. My crews and I have orchestrated the sinking of whaling ships in Iceland, Norway, Portugal, South Africa and Spain and crippled the operations of the largest whaling fleet of them all — the Japanese whalers in the Southern Ocean Whale Sanctuary.

Over these four decades of shutting down whaling operations, I found myself working in the same waters as the Confederate raiders did between 1861 and 1865. Where they hunted, we hunted. Where they found whalers, we found whalers. Where they had confrontations, we had confrontations. In the Bering Sea, the North Atlantic, off the coast of Africa and South America and in the South Pacific.

The history of the Confederate raiders, ships like the *Alabama*, the *Florida* and the *Shenandoah*, served as an inspiration, providing me with the coordinates of possible whaling operations, and most importantly of all, although this may seem strange, as a model for the strategic operational approach that I developed called aggressive nonviolence.

What the Confederate raiders and Sea Shepherd have in common is that not a single whaler was ever killed or wounded by our actions. The other thing we have in common is that we shut down whaling operations and sank whalers. The only real difference is that we intervened with the intention to save the lives of whales whereas the Confederates intervened for another reason altogether, yet with the same result of saving the lives of whales.

I decided to write this book after coming across a log entry by Cornelius E. Hunt, the Master's Mate of the Confederate raider **Shenandoah**. After boarding the Yankee whaler **Abigail** in the Okhotsk Sea in the month of May 1865, the whaling captain, Ebenezer Nye, resignedly said to Lieutenant Dabney Scales, "Well, I s'pose I'm taken! But who on earth would have thought of seeing one of your Southern privateers up here in the Okhotsk Sea. I heard of some of your pranks you fellows have been playing, but I supposed I was out of your reach."

Scales amusingly replied, "Why the fact of the business is, Captain, we have entered into a treaty offensive and defensive with the whales and are up here by special agreement to disperse their mortal enemies."

Of course, the Confederates were not actually sympathetic to the plight of the whales, but in practise what they did was to cripple the entire Yankee whaling fleet just when the whalers were on the threshold of obliterating many remaining whale populations.

The destruction of so many whaling ships bought time, and shortly after the Civil War in 1870, Rockefeller's discovery of how to refine petroleum into inexpensive fuel negated the market for expensive whale oil.

The Yankee whaling industry never recovered, especially after suffering two more great tragedies in 1871 and 1876.

Whaling, however, continued, but the war had indeed bought some time, allowing some whale populations to recover until the twentieth century, when the Norwegians began to industrialize the carnage, resulting in other nations like Great Britain, Germany, Russia and Japan, amongst others, waging yet another vicious war of extermination upon the world's whales, a slaughter so savagely merciless that in 1946, the International Whaling Commission (IWC) was established to regulate rules and quotas just to protect the industry from its own greed.

In 1974, as a young man of 23, I joined with many other conservationists to begin pressuring the IWC into adapting conservation measures for the protection of whales for the benefit of the whales and not just for the whaling industry. In 1982 the IWC implemented a global moratorium on commercial whaling that took effect in 1986 and remains in effect to the present day.

Despite this landmark decision, since 1986 the whalers of Japan, Norway and Iceland have slain over 33,000 whales in blatant defiance of the moratorium, and in the case of Japan, in blatant defiance of the International Court of Justice.

I became actively involved in 1974, preparing for my position as the first officer on the first Greenpeace voyage to save the whales. We confronted the North Pacific Soviet whaling fleet in June 1975 in a campaign that changed my entire outlook on life and set me on a steady course of dedicating the rest of my life to defending whales and other marine species.

During the month of June 1975, I had an experience that changed my life forever. The first Greenpeace voyage to defend the whales set out to intercept the Soviet whaling fleet. We had been reading quite a bit about Mahatma Gandhi and naively thought that we could non-violently block the harpoons with our bodies.

Robert Hunter and I found ourselves in a RIB, in front of a large Soviet harpoon vessel bearing down on us at full speed in rough seas, and before us were eight magnificent Sperm whales fleeing for their lives. Every time the harpooner tried to take a shot, I maneuvered our small inflatable boat to block his shot. That tactic worked for about 20 minutes until a very angry Soviet whaling captain came running down the catwalk to yell into the ear of the harpooner. He then turned and smiled down at us as he raked a finger across his throat.

A few moments later the harpooner fired over our heads with a thundering clap. The explosive-tipped harpoon whistled over our heads as the cable slashed the water beside us.

The missile struck a female in the pod. She screamed and rolled on her side, bleeding profusely. Suddenly the largest whale in the pod smacked his fluke upon the surface of the sea and disappeared beneath the surface as he turned completely around and swam directly underneath of us, rocketing to the surface before the Soviet vessel in a fruitless effort to defend his pod.

But the bastards were ready for him. The harpooner had quickly loaded an unattached harpoon and at point blank range fired a second shot at the huge head of the bull Sperm whale. He bellowed a horrific scream and fell back into the sea, rolling in agony on a surface turned scarlet red with his own blood.

As he writhed in agony, I caught his eye. He turned and dove, and I saw a trail of bloody bubbles coming straight before me. Suddenly he shot straight out of the water at an angle that would bring his huge body crashing down on our small boat. As his head rose higher out of the dark shroud of the sea, I could see the large teeth in the lower jaw. What I saw next changed the course of my life.

I was looking into his saucer-sized eye, so close I could see my own reflection, and in the depths of that solitary eye, I saw understanding. That whale understood what we had been trying to do. How, I don't know, this but I could see the great effort he made to pull himself back. His body began to slip beneath the swells. I saw his eye fall into the darkness, and he was gone.

He could have killed us but he did not. I owed my life to that whale, but I also felt something else. It was pity. Not for himself, but for us that we could take life so recklessly, without empathy or comprehension of what they were doing. And for what? One of the products that the Soviets lusted for was spermaceti oil, and one of the uses for that oil was to lubricate the mechanisms of Inter-Continental Ballistic Missiles. (ICBM's).

As the sun was setting, I sat in that tiny little boat on the dark high seas and I was struck by the realization that we humans were killing these highly intelligent, socially complex, self-aware sentient beings for the purpose of building a weapon meant for the purpose of the mass extermination of human beings.

It was at that moment I came to the realization that humanity was ecologically insane. I decided then and there to dedicate myself to saving the lives of whales. From that day on, they became my clients.

After working on three Greenpeace campaigns against the Soviet whalers, I grew frustrated with the Greenpeace approach of bearing witness and not intervening, of taking pictures and hanging banners. I felt there was a need for a more aggressive approach, but I also understood that to be successful, we still had to be strategically non-violent in our approach.

In 1977, I left Greenpeace and established the Sea Shepherd Conservation Society. It was not to be a protest group. I intended it to be an anti-poaching organization.

It was that year that I came across the Memoirs of Lieutenant Commander James Iredell Waddell of the Confederate raider *Shenandoah*.

It was Captain Waddell, along with Captains Raphael Semmes of the *Alabama* and Captain John Newland Maffitt of the *Florida,* who provided me with the blueprint to organize an aggressive yet non-violent strategy to intervene and destroy illegal whaling operations.

I employed their logs to locate whaling grounds and I tailored some of their tactics to stop the whalers. The major difference between the Confederate raiders and my ships, of course, aside from motivation, was guns. The raiders were heavily armed and very intimidating. It was this intimidation that was their greatest strength. Fortunately, I was able to find a way to be intimidating and effective without being armed.

The crews of the raiders and my crews also had a few virtues in common despite our completely different causes.

In researching this book, I was struck by the fact that during my forty-four years of voyages to defend whales, my path crossed that of the Confederate raiders many times. I saw the places they saw, sailed the same waters they sailed and visited many of the same ports.

We have also had similar experiences. Whereas the United States Navy was expending considerable resources to stop the Confederates, the Japanese government and whalers had invested considerable

xviii The War That Saved the Whales

resources to try to stop us from interfering with their whaling operations. And by coincidence, the same port of Williamstown in Victoria, Australia, where the *Shenandoah* was drydocked in 1864 is the same port that serves as our base of operations today in our efforts to oppose the Japanese whalers in the Southern Ocean.

I have sailed through the same Southern Pacific islands as the *Shenandoah* and also voyaged deep into the Bering Sea and the Arctic Ocean to defend whales. I landed on St. Lawrence Island in the Bering Sea in 1981 and met with the descendants of the same Yupik people who had greeted and traded with the *Shenandoah's* crew in June 1865.

I have worked with the Brazilian rangers to patrol for poachers at Fernando de Noronha island off the coast of Brazil, the same island where Captain Rafael Semmes landed prisoners from the *Alabama* and I have also made port at Gibraltar, Brest, France, Nassau, and other places where the raiders frequented.

The Confederate raiders and my Sea Shepherd ships shared a common objective although for completely different reasons. The raiders were intent upon destroying Yankee commerce and Yankee whaling as a means of undermining the Union economically. They were commerce raiders. They bore no grudge against the whalers themselves, just their flag, but the result was positive for the whales, and thus I very much appreciate what they were able to accomplish.

For myself it is the whalers who are the enemy, not their flag, and I have intervened and confronted whalers from Japan, the former Soviet Union, Norway, Iceland, Spain, Australia, South Africa and even the Makah Indian tribe of the United States.

These Confederate buccaneers passionately fought for what they believed in, courageously exercising resourcefulness to utilize their imaginations to overcome difficult and challenging obstacles.

Their cause, of course, was wrong and thankfully for humanity they lost, but in doing so they achieved something extremely positive for the entire world. It was not their intention, but the results can now be very much appreciated.

I am convinced that without their intervention between the years 1861 and 1865 that five species of whales could have been driven close to extinction.

The Bowhead, the Right whales, the Humpback, the Sperm and the Pacific Gray were coveted targets of the New England whalers. How many more of them would have died had their persecutors not been destroyed is unknown, but it is safe to say that the number would have been many thousands.

Thankfully these species were able to slowly recover from the brink of extinction, although they continued to be threatened by the thoughtlessness and greed of humanity.

The actions of the Confederate raiders are not generally known today. To many then, as now, these men are often regarded as lawless pirates, failed racist insurgents and terrorists. To me, however, they were inspiring heroes.

In saying this I am taking these men out of the context of the cause they were fighting for. My focus is on what they contributed to the cause of protecting whales. In this one thing they are indeed heroes, although unwittingly, for they had no comprehension of the positive contribution they were making to marine conservation.

Fortunately, they lost the war, they took no lives and they saved thousands of whales, and thus the American Civil War can legitimately be called the "War That Helped to Save the Whales."

CHAPTER I

War & Whales

The history of modern human warfare has been a double-edged sword for the nation of cetaceans.

Destruction of whalers and cessation of whaling were the benefits to the whales of the American Revolution, in the War of 1812 by the American and the British fleets against each other's whaling operations, the American Civil War and World Wars I & II.

On the other hand, the demand for whale oil was greatly increased by the Great War of 1914–1918 for the manufacture of nitroglycerin. Glycerol was produced from animal fats by treating the fats with alkalis like ash from burnt seaweed. Thousands of tons of whale fat and oil were used for the manufacture of high explosives.

It is rather strange to realize that the men dying on the bloody muddy fields of France were being ripped apart by materials obtained by savagely ripping apart the bodies of sentient innocent whales in the sea.

Such is the insanity of humanity.

Over 8.5 million soldiers died on the Western Front between 1914 and 1918 in good part because of an invention by Alfred Nobel, who began manufacturing dynamite in 1907. And thus, it is stranger still that this man who contributed so much to the death both of whales and humans now has a peace prize presented every year in his name.

In order to feed the insatiable appetite of the God of War to consume human lives in both great wars, some 50,000 whales were slaughtered every year for the first half of the twentieth century to provide the lethal materials.

Whale oil was used also to grease the wet feet of soldiers in the trenches to prevent trench foot. A battalion of a thousand men would use 10 gallons of whale oil every day to grease their feet, and there were many battalions on both sides of the trenches.

Sperm whale oil was also highly coveted for oiling the parts of Intercontinental Ballistic Missiles.

In many various ways, whales were ruthlessly slaughtered for the murderous sins of humans against other humans. These incredibly intelligent self-aware sentient beings died in vast numbers simply because of the violent tendencies and stupidity of Homo sapiens.

By 1860, the world's whales had already endured a relentless assault for centuries. The peak of Yankee slaughter was reached in the 1840s. Whale populations were greatly diminished and their migratory routes widely disrupted.

The whaling fleets were forced to go further and further away in pursuit of their prey. They chased the Sperm in the waters of the Azores and across the South Pacific. The slow-moving Right whales were decimated from the coast of New England down to Patagonia. The blubber hunters harassed the Humpbacks from Hawaii north to the Aleutians and reached even further north into the Okhotsk Sea and to the high Arctic in pursuit of the Grays and the Bowheads.

The slaughter was remorseless, relentless and cruel.

It was ironic that out of the vicious sibling conflict between the Northern and the Southern States, the forces defending human slavery would devastate the Quaker industry of whaling and be the cause of saving so many cetacean lives, and it is entirely possible that the Confederate raiders did even more than save lives. Perhaps without their intervention, the Bowheads, the Rights, the Grays and the Humpbacks would have been driven into extinction.

There was absolutely no concept of conservation in the mid–nineteenth century. Hardly a thought was given in New Bedford or

Nantucket to the survival of the whales. The Quakers saw only one thing and that was profit from as much oil as they could extract as quickly as possible.

The world's living oil industry of the day was insatiable, and it was not only the whales that suffered. On Australia's MacQuairie Island, live penguins were tossed into the boiling trypots to extract what little oil they could render. Seals, sea elephants and sea lions all found their way into the evil iron pots. The streetlights of New York, Boston, London and San Francisco and so many other cities flickered with the bodily fluids from millions of sentient beings whose lives were savagely extinguished by harpoons and lances.

In 1847 the first Bowheads were killed in the Sea of Okhotsk by a Danish whaler. This immediately attracted the interest of the New England whalers and in 1848, Captain Thomas Welcome Roys of Sag Harbour sailed into the area with his bark *Superior* to begin the Yankee slaughter. Within a year another 49 Yankee whalers were in the Sea of Okhotsk. By the time of the outbreak of the Civil War in 1860, more than a hundred and fifty whalers were chasing down every Bowhead whale they could see in these same waters.

In 1865 when the *Shenandoah* entered the Sea of Okhotsk, they found only one whaling ship, the luckless *Abigail*, whose skipper Ebenezer Nye complained that there were few whales to be found.

Between 1847 and 1865, some 18,000 Bowheads had been slaughtered with some 80 percent of that number killed by 1855. The massacre of Bowheads was almost complete in the Sea of Okhotsk, which is why the *Shenandoah* captured only the one whaler during a month of cruising.

Captain James Waddell did discover from the charts on the *Abigail* that the Yankee whaling fleet had moved north to the Bering Straits.

There, in the waters between St. Lawrence Island to the south and the Diomede Islands to the north, the slaughter continued without mercy. An estimated 18,600 Bowheads were slain between 1858 and 1914, and 60% of that number had been killed by the time the *Shenandoah* found itself amidst the whalers.

Today less than 400 extremely endangered Bowheads survive in the Sea of Okhotsk, and Bowhead populations elsewhere are considered endangered and threatened.

The Yankee whalers pursued the Humpbacks in the Atlantic, the Pacific and the Indian Ocean, and the Confederate raider interventions definitely saved a large number of this species.

The *Shenandoah* also cut into the number of Pacific Gray whales taken, a population that was nearly exterminated by 1900.

It is amazing that the great whale species managed to survive to this day. Their gene pool has been diminished, their habitats ravaged and the industrialized slaughter of the twentieth century was horrific, and still to this day the killing continues by Japan, Iceland and Norway. Bowheads continue to be killed by the Yupik and the Inuit.

Since 1975 I have intervened against whaling operations fully aware of the bloody history of my own species against these incredibly intelligent, socially complex, self-aware sentient beings. Looking back over the history of human cetacean relationships, the only times prior to 1975 that humans actually but unintentionally defended the whales were the brief periods that humans were intent upon destroying each other. By the British against the Yankee fleets during the American Revolution and in the war of 1812, by the Germans against the British and Norwegian whaling fleet in WWII and by the Confederate Navy between 1861 and 1865.

The British Navy crippled the Yankee whalers during the American revolution and again during the War of 1812, blockading the whaling ships and keeping them in port.

"During three and a half years I remained at my native place, could do little. Our coasts and harbours were blockaded, and we at Nantucket lay at the mercy of our friends and enemies."

— Captain Edmund Gardner – during the War of 1812.

The War of 1812 was beneficial for the whales on both sides. In January 1813, the American ship *Essex* under the command of Captain David Porter decimated the British whaling fleet in the South Pacific. At the same time, British warships were destroying Yankee whalers in the same waters.

The War of 1812 crippled the New England whaling industry until 1820, when the great age of Yankee whaling began. It lasted until 1865, and it was a combination of diminished whale numbers and the predations of the Confederate raiders that put an end to it.

During WWII, the German commerce raider *Pinguin* captured an entire Norwegian whaling fleet of 15 ships, knocking them out of action for the duration of the war.

The fleet was captured near South Georgia Island: two factory ships, the *Ole Wegger* (12,201 tons) and the *Pelagos* (12,083 ton) the supply ship *Solglimt* (12,246 ton) and eleven harpoon vessels.

The *Pinguin* led the 14 captured ships to the Kerguelen Islands, where the cargos of whale oil and fuel oil were transferred to German cargo ships. The two factory ships and the supply vessel and nine of the harpoon vessels were then dispatched to Bordeaux. One harpoon boat, the *Pol IX*, was converted to an auxiliary vessel and two, the *Star XIX* and the Star *XXIV*, were sunk enroute to Bordeaux by the German prize crews to keep from being recaptured by the British naval vessel *HMS Scarborough.*

The *Pinguin* was the most successful of all commerce raiders when it came to stopping whaling operations. Not a single whaler was killed during these successful operations.

The crew of the *Pinguin* were not so fortunate. On May 8, 1941, the German commerce raider and HMS *Cornwall* faced off in a violent exchange that resulted in the deaths of 341 German crew and 214 of her prisoners.

It was the end of a career that had sunk or captured 28 ships and covered 59,000 nautical miles over 357 days at sea.

In 2010, my ship the *Steve Irwin* arranged a rendezvous with Captain Alex Cornelissen's *Bob Barker* at the French Kerguelen Islands, one of the most remote island groups in the world in the southern

Indiana Ocean, to transfer supplies and fuel. We were on our way to challenge the Japanese whaling fleet. In 2013 our three ships the **Steve Irwin**, the **Bob Barker** and the **Sam Simon** stopped briefly in the Kerguelen Islands.

As I looked across the bay towards the green treeless hills, I could picture the German commerce raider and her captive fleet nestled in the very same bay, and here it was less than a century later and whaling ships were still going about their grisly business.

It has always been my understanding that history is most useful as a guide for actions in the present. We learn from the mistakes and the successes of the past. In order to fight whalers in my lifetime, I needed to know how others fought whalers in the past.

CHAPTER II

First Blood

December 8, 1861

On December 20, 1860, South Carolina seceded from the Union of the United States of America. According to her leaders, she had every right to do so and other Southern states agreed. Within seven weeks, six more states seceded, and these seven rebellious states together drafted a provisional constitution to create the Confederate States of America. They also elected their first and only president, Jefferson Davis.

The Federal fortress in Charleston Harbor refused to submit to the Confederacy. In retaliation, South Carolina fired upon Fort Sumter, beginning the hostilities that rapidly evolved into the War between the States.

After the fall of Fort Sumter, four more states joined the Confederacy seeking independence from what they considered the tyranny of Northern aggression.

Today, most people regard the American Civil War as a war against slavery. That was not the way the North or the South regarded it at the beginning of the conflict.

Southerners believed they were fighting for independence from an aggressive North. In the North it was regarded as the putting down of a treasonous rebellion. There was not much discussion of slavery at first. Abraham Lincoln said to New York publisher Horace Greeley in 1862, "My paramount object in this struggle is to save the Union, and is not either to save or to destroy slavery."

The Proclamation of Emancipation came two years later more as a tactical decision than a humanitarian one.

The agrarian South had little manufacturing capability. The call to arms was motivated out of idealism and fired by passion. The impracticality of their cause would not stand in the way of their desire to cut all political ties with the North.

The South had always argued that the conflict was over the rights of the individual states, whereas the North has always advanced the nobility of anti-slavery as the motivation for their aggression.

I have never accepted that the North entered the war to champion the cause of abolition. Abraham Lincoln himself had not issued any orders to free the slaves, and the reality of slavery in 1860 was that it no longer made any economic sense. The Northern states had developed a much more exploitive and cost-effective form of slavery.

Purchasing a slave was expensive, and once purchased, the slave had to be fed, clothed, housed and his or her health had to be looked after. In the North, men and women, boys and girls, were put to work in the mines, the mills, and the factories and paid less than a dollar a day. They were then responsible for their own meals, clothing, and housing; and if sick or injured, they could be discarded without any need for the boss to provide medical care. In many cases they were simply worked to an early death.

The writing was on the wall, and for the South to compete, slavery would have had to go. It was only a matter of time, and most likely slavery would have ended in the South by 1875 if left to die a natural economic death.

What is evident is that the South was facing superior odds both in wealth and manufacturing capability.

The South did nonetheless have an army and skilled military leaders. What they did not have was a navy.

The Northern states entered the war with forty-two commissioned ships and an additional forty-eight in preparation for mobilization. The war would catapult the Union Navy into becoming the most powerful naval force in the world, surpassing the imperial

British Navy, which up until then had been the most powerful naval force to ever rule the waves.

And the Union Navy wasted little time in directing its naval forces to blockade the Southern ports in an effort to restrict trade and commerce between the Southern States and other nations, especially the European nations.

The Union initiated a campaign to devastate the South economically by striking at the ability of the Confederacy to export cotton and other goods, and to import weapons and supplies.

The South retaliated in kind with one of the most effective naval strategies of the war. With never more than eight ships and four tenders, and with never more than two cruisers under command at any one time, the South built up a strategy to cripple Northern maritime commerce and ended up practically destroying the Yankee whaling fleet.

But the South did not do it alone. Without British complicity, the strategy of undermining Yankee maritime commerce could not have been pulled off. Great Britain had a very practical vested interest in seeing the South succeed.

Great Britain was staunchly anti-slavery, but they also saw the opportunity to cut down their competition. By 1860, the United States merchant fleet was transporting over 70% of all worldwide trade and doing it faster and cheaper than the British. The British also had a demand for Southern cotton and tobacco, and the Union blockades were causing the prices of these two commodities to rise significantly.

President Jefferson Davis appointed Stephen R. Mallory as Secretary of the Confederate Navy on March 18, 1861, and Mallory was more than capable of taking on this responsibility.

Mallory knew that he could never compete with his Northern counterpart Gideon Welles. He did not have the capability to build ships or even to forge guns. He focused on converting the 3,200 ton, twin-engine *Merrimack* into an ironclad to oppose blockade vessels, and it was very successful. Unfortunately for the South, due to the recapture of Norfolk by Major General George B. McClellan's Army of the Potomac and the defeat of the **Merrimack** by the Union ironclad the **Monitor,** Confederate Naval power practically ceased to exist.

The South was losing badly to the American Navy. By the end of the war, the Union ships would seize or destroy some 1,500 blockade runners.

Mallory did not have ships, but he had superb men to command them. He just needed to find ships to command.

On February 14, 1861, a letter arrived in Mobile, Alabama to a former United States Naval commander named Raphael Semmes.

Montgomery, Feb 14, 1862

Sir: On behalf of the Committee on Naval Affairs, I beg leave to request that you repair to this place, at your earliest convenience.

Your O.B. Servant
C.M. Conrad

Raphael Semmes resigned his commission in the U.S. Navy and reported to Montgomery four days later.

Semmes tried to purchase vessels in the North and in Canada but found it not practical, and soon had Federal agents on his trail. He retreated to New Orleans and there was given the task of refitting an old bark rigged schooner into a warship. The vessel was the **Havana,** and she had been used to ferry passengers between New Orleans and Cuba.

Semmes had her re-rigged to a barkentine, the frames strengthened, the passenger cabins removed, and a magazine built. He also expanded the bunkers to carry eight days of coal. He armed the vessel with an eight-inch pivot gun and four thirty-two pounders, two on each side.

He named her the CSS **Sumter.** She was small, but she was the first commissioned Confederate warship, and Semmes had her made ready to begin an assault on Northern commerce.

As he made the **Sumter** ready for sea, he had the pick of the experienced sailors of New Orleans. He selected Lieutenant John

McIntosh Kell as his executive officer. He also selected Second Lieutenant George T. Chapman and Third Lieutenant John M. Stribling.
The fourth lieutenant selected was William E. Evans. The Marine
detachment was commanded by President Jefferson Davis's brother-
in-law, Lieutenant of Marines Becket K. Howell.

Semmes was very much satisfied with the officers he had selected
and wrote to Secretary Mallory, "Should I be fortunate enough to
reach the high seas, you may rely upon my implicit obedience of your
instructions, 'to do the enemy's commerce the greatest injury in the
shortest time.'"

Semmes boarded 22 officers, 72 seaman, and 20 marines.

But being ready for sea was one thing, and making it to sea
was something else altogether. New Orleans was blockaded by the
21-gun, 2,532-ton *Brooklyn*; the 16-gun, 3,765-ton *Powhatan*; the
32-gun, 4,582-ton *Niagara;* and the 53-gun, 3,307-ton *Minnesota*.
Semmes also knew that with a top speed of only 9 knots he would
not be able to outrun the faster Union ships.

The 437-ton *Sumter* would stand no chance against the Yankee
guns. Semmes had to find a way to avoid them to reach the sea.
It was not easy, and Semmes and his crew spent many blistering
days in the sweltering marshes of the Mississippi waiting for their
opportunity.

That opportunity arrived on the morning of June 30th, with a
report that the *Brooklyn* under the command of Captain Charles H.
Poor had left her post to chase a sail and was out of sight. Semmes
quickly hauled up his anchor and prepared to swing his ship into the
current of the Mississippi to head for the bar.

Semmes described it as a race, "which was to decide whether we
should continue to stagnate in mid-summer in the marshes of the
Mississippi or reach those glad waters of the dark blue sea."

As they made to enter the river, the pilot, a Northern sympathizer, claimed he knew nothing about the bar of the Pass a L'Outre.
An angry Semmes roared out to the man, "You take us out, damn
you, and if you run us ashore or put us into the hands of the enemy,
I shall swing you from the yardarm as a traitor."

And then they spied the **Brooklyn**; she had returned, four miles off and approaching very quickly. Semmes made the decision to run for the bar despite the untrustworthiness of his pilot. Suddenly a seaman shouted that a whaleboat was approaching with four strong black men pulling hard on the oars. In the stern of the boat sat a young pilot, and on the balcony of the pilot house stood an incredibly beautiful woman, the pilot's young wife, smiling as she waved him on with her handkerchief.

Semmes uncovered his head to his fellow country-woman and welcomed her husband on board.

Into the river she steamed, and a crowd cheered as the **Sumter** passed the lighthouse wharf, watching as the first of the Confederate raiders passed over the bar. As the pilot boat pulled alongside, the young pilot departed and shook Semmes's hand, saying, "Now Captain, you are all clear, give her hell and let her go!"

Over the bar they were, but the **Brooklyn** was still hot on her tail and she was a much faster ship. Semmes threw a howitzer overboard, dumped 1,500 tons of fresh water to lighten his vessel, and poured on the coal. Both ships headed with all the speed they could muster, with steam and sail towards the open sea and into a sudden rain-squall.

The rain-squall was followed by a breeze more favorable to the **Sumter,** and she gained slowly on the **Brooklyn.** Half an hour later, the Union ship abandoned the chase, allowing the **Sumter** to escape.

The first victim of the **Sumter,** intercepted on July 3, 1861, was the 607-ton **Golden Rocket** out of Brewer, Maine. Semmes informed the Yankee skipper, "My duty is a painful one to destroy so noble a ship as yours...for yourself, you will only have to do, as so many thousands have done before you, submit to the fortunes of war – yourself and your crew will be well treated on board my ship."

He then burned the **Golden Rocket,** igniting not just the ship, but the beginning of the reign of destruction by the Confederate raiders.

With the **Sumter,** Semmes out maneuvered and eluded the United States Navy for over six months. From Cuba to Curacao to Brazil, back to the Caribbean, to the North Atlantic, and over to Europe, keeping one step ahead of his Yankee pursuers.

Semmes had both courage and imagination, and was not adverse to doing the unexpected. When United States Consul Moses Jesurun threatened the governor of Curacao with reprisals if he allowed Semmes to re-coal, the governor issued an order demanding that the *Sumter* not enter or be granted entry to the Dutch port. Semmes responded by firing four shells over the Dutch government buildings, all bursting in the air, with the desired effect of the governor dispatching a boat with an invitation for Semmes to enter the port.

The U.S. Consul was furious but powerless to prevent the *Sumter* from repairs and provisions. He bribed some of the Confederate sailors for information and "discovered" that Semmes was heading north through the Mona Passage. Jesurun sent word to his superiors, unaware that Semmes constantly misinformed his crew of his intentions, trusting only Lieutenant Kell with his confidence. At no time did any of the officers or crew have any idea where the *Sumter* would head next, although most thought they did.

On Sea Shepherd campaigns, this was a valuable lesson for me, and I made it a policy to never divulge our course, and in many cases our destination, to my crew prior to departure.

Semmes headed towards Venezuela and Trinidad.

Ironically, one of Semmes's most enthusiastic pursuers was Captain David Dixson Porter on the USS *Powhatan*. Porter was a former shipmate of Semmes, and his father was Commodore David Porter, who had destroyed the British whaling fleet in the Pacific in 1813 when he was Captain of the U.S. frigate *Essex*.

Fortunately for the whales and for the Confederacy, Porter did not have the same success with the *Sumter* that his father had with the British whalers. Try as he might, he was unable to capture Semmes, although he did come as close as 40 miles of the *Sumter* in the dark of night. Everywhere that Porter thought Semmes would head, the *Sumter* went somewhere else. As Porter scoured the Caribbean, Semmes sailed south to the coast of Suriname.

When word reached Porter and the other Union ships from Suriname, Semmes headed to Brazil. He lingered at Sao Luis and left just in time, with Porter arriving four days later. Within two weeks he had captured and burned the *Joseph Park*, a merchant vessel.

In the 45 days since leaving Brazil, the *Sumter* had only burned two vessels, but from capturing and releasing fifteen neutrals, he learned that his efforts had caused merchants to forsake consigning cargoes to American vessels. The U.S. merchant fleet was beginning to feel the economic pressure this one small Rebel raider was costing them.

The Union Navy was desperate to destroy the *Sumter.*

On November 9th, Captain Semmes came dangerously close to being captured when he dropped anchor at Fort de France in Martinique. Semmes was on good terms with Governor Maussion de Cande, who was a Rear Admiral in the French Navy. This irritated U.S. Consul John Campbell greatly because he was unable to prevent the *Sumter* from purchasing coal and provisions. On November 13th, the *Sumter* took on water and coal and had a further delay for repairs to the boiler.

Semmes knew it was dangerous to linger, but he had no choice. The repairs were a necessity. And so, it was not a great surprise when the 8-gun sloop *Iroquois* arrived outside of the harbor on the 14th.

United States Naval Captain James S. Palmer believed he had the Confederate raider in a trap that she could not escape. For ten days the *Sumter* remained in the harbor with every day bringing the possibility of the arrival of additional Union ships.

It was a difficult situation. The *Iroquois* was twice the size and three knots faster than the *Sumter,* and she had bigger guns. A U.S. merchant ship in the harbor kept the *Iroquois* informed of any movements by the *Sumter* with signal lights. The U.S. Consul also arranged for signals to be sent from shore to the Union warship.

Semmes studied the signals and waited for a dark night to make his play. In the early evening of November 23rd, Executive Officer Kell organized the crew. They quietly hoisted the anchor and cut the stern cables. They could see the *Iroquois's* outline at a distance outside the harbor as they quietly slipped past the French warship *Acheron*. The French sailors gave a quiet cheer and hand signals of good luck. Watching the signals, Semmes noticed the merchant ship telling the *Iroquois* that the *Sumter* was moving south. He quickly reversed and headed to the north end of the island.

In his log, Semmes wrote, "It is safe to say that the next morning the two vessels were one hundred and fifty miles apart! …The signals were of vast service to me."

And he was just in time. The next morning saw the arrival of the USS *Dacotah* and eight other Union warships were now on the hunt for him in the Caribbean.

Needless to say, Naval Secretary Gideon Welles was not happy with Captain Palmer and relieved him of his command, although he did reinstate him four months later.

But escape Semmes did, and now he was in the open Atlantic and heading towards Europe. On the way he bonded the merchant vessel *Montmorenci* and released her because of her neutral cargo, and he caught and burned the schooner *Arcade* loaded with barrel staves and bound for Guadeloupe.

On December 3rd the *Sumter* chased down the 1,100-ton *Vigilant* some 400 miles south of Bermuda, much to the surprise of her captain and crew. They had newspapers onboard reporting that the *Iroquois* had the *Sumter* trapped at Martinique.

Semmes burned the *Vigilant* and headed east towards Spain.

Between July 3 and December 3, 1861, the *Sumter* captured fifteen ships, burning five of them, and bonding or releasing the rest.

On December 8th, the *Sumter* intercepted her first and only whaler.

The bark *Ebenezer Dodge* out of New Bedford had the distinction of being the first whaling ship put to the torch by the Confederate raiders, and the only whaler destroyed out of the seven vessels burned by the CSS *Sumter* under the command of Captain Raphael Semmes.

The unlucky whaler was only twelve days out of New Bedford and bound for the Pacific whaling grounds when Raphael Semmes intercepted her.

It had not been a pleasant twelve days for the crew of the *Ebenezer Dodge*. The old bark had been severely battered by an Atlantic storm and was just recovering that very morning. She was still leaking badly when the *Sumter* approached at around 10:00 hours from out of the fog.

The *Sumter* fired a ball across the bow of the whaler and hoisted the American flag. The *Ebenezer Dodge* did the same, feeling relieved to see the star-spangled banner. As they came alongside, the American flag was lowered from the *Sumter* and the Stars and Bars abruptly raised, much to the shock of the whaling crew.

The Southerners had put to sea clad only in summer clothing and were quite pleased to seize the warm clothing from the whaler, which was well supplied with boots, flannels, and pea jackets.

Twenty-two whalers were taken prisoner and these, added to prisoners already onboard, brought the number of captives to forty-three.

The *Ebenezer Dodge* had just barely escaped confiscation for the great stone fleet and had been outfitted by her owner Benjamin Franklin Howland for a whaling venture to the Pacific.

The ship had departed from New Bedford on November 25th under the command of Captain Gideon C. Hoxie. His instructions were to take the old bark round Cape Horn with the mission of scouring the South Pacific for three years in search of whales.

Captain Hoxie and his crew would not be rounding the Horn, numerous whales would be spared their cruel harpoons, and the whaler *Ebenezer Dodge* would have the distinction of being the first whaler since the War of 1812 to be seized and destroyed by an enemy upon the high seas.

It would not be the last whaler so condemned.

Captain Semmes examined the papers presented to him by Captain Hoxie and calmly said to him, "Oh yes, it's all right. She is a lawful prize of the Confederate States, and I shall burn the ship. We are short of water and you have plenty; I must have some of that."

Captain Hoxie offered no resistance. What could he do? Armed against defenseless whales with lances, and harpoons, small bombs, and firearms, a whaler could be boastfully brave. Against a fully armed man of war, well, that was something else altogether.

In addition to the warm clothing and a thousand gallons of fresh water, the Confederates seized tobacco, charts, carpenter's tools, a sextant and a chronometer and two excellent whale boats in addition to provisions.

With his ship crowded with prisoners, the whalers were forced to bed down on the decks. This was cause to lament that from the beginning their voyage was jinxed to one of exceptionally bad luck as the *Sumter* headed into yet another severe Atlantic gale.

At the time of the burning of the *Ebenezer Dodge*, Semmes had not been aware of the Great Stone Fleet; for if he had he would have had real cause to be angry with the whalers. As it was, although he had just destroyed his first whaling vessel, he had a begrudging respect for the Yankee whalers.

He had written that he believed that New England supremacy in whaling was derived "from the superior skill, energy, industry, courage, and perseverance of the Yankee whaler, who is, perhaps, the best specimen of a sailor, the world over."

But his opinion aside, the Yankees were the enemy, and the *Ebenezer Dodge* was put to the torch at 18:30 hours in the deteriorating weather. Through the drizzle, Semmes along with Captain Hoxie, both with vastly different emotions, watched as the flames were energized by the sperm oil-soaked wood into a spectacular bonfire.

As the dancing orange flames ravaged and engulfed the whaler, Semmes said it reminded him of a jack-o-lantern.

Captain Hoxie did not say a word as the distance between the *Sumter* and the doomed *Ebenezer Dodge* widened and the dancing lights disappeared over the horizon.

The *Sumter's* career as a raider was ended when mechanical difficulties forced her into the port of Gibraltar. Her boilers needed replacement. Forced to remain in Gibraltar, it did not take long before Union warships arrived to prevent her departure. Semmes abandoned her, leaving only a couple of officers onboard, a decision that forced the Union to continue their stations for six months tying up the Union ships *Tuscarora, Ino, Constellation* and *Kearsarge* waiting for the departure of a vessel Semmes no longer commanded nor intended to put to sea again.

After abandoning the *Sumter*, Raphael Semmes returned to the Southern States. From there he was given instructions to depart for the Bahamas and from there on to Great Britain.

I abandoned my ship the *Sea Shepherd II* at Ucluelet on Vancouver Island in the summer of 1992 after being ordered into port by Canadian authorities, intent upon harassment. They ordered me to pay a fee, which I refused, and when told the ship could not depart without the payment of the fee, I decided to abandon the vessel because I already had plans to retire the ship because of her age. My abandoned ship was cause for many regrets by the Canadian government over the next decade.

An important part of strategy is knowing when to walk away and knowing when to abandon your ship.

CHAPTER III

The Destruction of the Sierra

July, 1979, Portugal

In early July of 1979, I put into the port of Horta on the island of Fayal on my way to hunt down the pirate whaler *Sierra*. I was forced to discharge two crew members after they became drunk and disorderly while on shore, one of them having become so inclined to violence when he had returned to my ship the *Sea Shepherd*, I was forced to march him down the gangplank at the point of a sword.

The reason for my impatience with the two drunk seamen is that the night before, I had taken an axe to some of the Azorean whale boats on the beach, leaving each with a large hole below their water line. The last thing I needed was suspicion to fall upon us because of the two unruly drunks.

Fortunately, the damages were not discovered before we departed. As we cruised eastward, we passed numerous Sperm whales and I told the crew how 117 years before, the *Alabama* had driven the Yankee whalers from these waters and brought relative peace to the Sperm whale breeding grounds until at least 1866.

The 1861–1865 voyages of the *Sumter, Alabama, Florida,* and *Shenandoah* have been an inspiration for me for many years. I despise whaling ships, and reading about ships dedicated to the destruction of these vessels of death has given me immense pleasure.

I also admired the Confederate Captains and their restraint in not causing a single injury to the whaling men they captured. They destroyed their industry without taking their lives, and I found that very inspiring.

On July 15, 1979, I had found the pirate whaler *Sierra* and began to give chase. Chase her I did, for two hundred miles and into the Portuguese port of Leixoes.

There in the harbor I came at her at full speed and rammed her bow to damage her harpoon. I then came about and hit her full speed midship, splitting her open to the waterline and ending her grisly outlaw career.

The Portuguese Navy gave chase and brought us back to Leixoes, and I was charged with gross criminal negligence by the port captain. However, I explained that there was nothing negligent about what we did at all, because we had struck the *Sierra* precisely where we intended to strike her, and thus being deliberate, it was not negligent.

The Port Captain laughed and had to agree with my boast, adding that they could not find out who actually owned the *Sierra* and that until they did, I was free to leave.

My ship was ordered tied up in the inner harbor. The *Sierra* was moved to Lisbon to undergo extensive repairs.

Although none of us were charged, my ship was ordered confiscated by the local court without a hearing. We were told that the owner of the *Sierra*, a South African named Andrew Behr, had bribed the judge and that the ship would be turned over to him as compensation for the damages that we had caused to the *Sierra*.

I was not going to have my ship turned over to a whaler. During the evening of December 31st, my Chief Engineer Peter Woof and I boarded the *Sea Shepherd* and scuttled her in the harbor.

New Year's Day of 1980 saw firemen, police, and Portuguese soldiers scouring the docks as hundreds of citizens flocked down to the harbor to see my ship, her stern on the bottom and her bow pointing skyward. It was a sad sight, but it was necessary. I would not have her in the hands of the whalers.

On February 6, 1980, after expensive repairs and on the eve of her plans to return to killing whales, we sank the *Sierra* dockside in Lisbon Harbor.

On April 28, 1980, we sank the Spanish whalers *Isba Uno* and *Isba Duo* in the same way in Marin Harbor near Vigo, Spain.

In June of 2010 I arrived at the island of Madeira to attend the International Whaling Commission meeting. I had been to Portugal, the Azores and Madeira a few times since 1979 without any incident, but this time the Japanese government pressured the Portuguese government to look into my past. I found myself detained at the airport and told that there was a warrant out for my arrest.

After being detained for six hours, I was informed that the warrant was for the ramming of the whaler *Sierra* in 1979.

"Does this mean you intend to arrest me?" I asked the immigration officer.

He smiled and said, "It turns out that the warrant expired a month ago, so you are free to enter Madeira."

Needless to say, the Japanese delegation to the International Whaling Commission was not happy to see me arrive at the hotel where the annual meeting was taking place.

Whereas the Yankee whaler *Ebenezer Dodge* was the first whaler destroyed by the Confederate raider *Sumter*, the Cypriot registered *Sierra* was my first kill.

Not a single crew member on the *Sierra* or the two Spanish whalers was injured.

The *Sumter* sank only the one whaler, but she was the ship upon whose decks Captain Raphael Semmes began his illustrious career of destroying Yankee commerce ships and—most importantly for myself – whaling ships.

The *Sumter's* career as a raider was ended when mechanical difficulties forced her into the port of Gibraltar. Her boilers needed replacement. Forced to remain in Gibraltar, it did not take long before Union warships arrived to prevent her departure. Semmes abandoned her, leaving only a couple of officers onboard, a decision that forced the Union to continue their stations for six months tying up the Union ships *Tuscarora, Ino, Constellation* and *Kearsarge* waiting for the departure of a vessel Semmes no longer commanded nor intended to put to sea again.

After abandoning the *Sumter*, Raphael Semmes returned to the Southern States. From there he was given instructions to depart for the Bahamas and from there on to Great Britain.

I abandoned my ship the *Sea Shepherd II* at Ucluelet on Vancouver Island in the summer of 1992 after being ordered into port by Canadian authorities, intent upon harassment. They ordered me to pay a fee which I refused and when told the ship could not depart without the payment of the fee, I decided to abandon the vessel because I already had plans to retire the ship because of her age. My abandoned ship was cause for many regrets by the Canadian government over the next decade.

An important part of strategy is knowing when to walk away and knowing when to abandon your ship.

Chapter IV

The Great Stone Fleet

In 1861, Herman Melville wrote a poem about one of the most unusual fleets to ever set sail upon the high seas. A fleet whose planned destiny was to be sunk in its entirety, yet without loss of life. A fleet that put to sea at high cost, yet accomplished nothing strategic, nothing that is for those who were in command. However, much was indeed accomplished for the nation of whales, for most of the Stone Fleet were whalers and their loss was one of the most positive outcomes for the oceans and the whales from any human conflict in history, save only the destruction brought down on the heads of the whalers by the Confederate raiders.

Together the Confederate raiders and their Yankee foes broke the backbone of the Yankee whaling industry to the point that it never fully recovered.

The Stone Fleet --- An Old Sailor's Lament
(December, 1861)
Herman Melville

I have a feeling for those ships,
Each worn and ancient one,
With great bluff bows, and broad in the beam:
Ay, it was unkindly done.
But so they serve the Obsolete —
Even so, Stone Fleet!

You'll say I'm doting; do but think
I scudded round the Horn in one —
The Tenedos, a glorious
Good old craft as ever run —
Sunk (how all unmeet!)
With the Old Stone Fleet.

An India ship of fame was she,
Spices and shawls and fans she bore;
A whaler when her wrinkles came —
Turned off! Till, spent and poor,
Her bones were sold (escheat)!
Ah! Stone Fleet.

Four were erst patrician keels
(Names attest what families be),
The Kensington, and Richmond too,
Leonidas, and Lee:
But now they have their seat
With the Old Stone Fleet.

To scuttle them — a pirate deed —
Sack them, and dismast;
They sunk so slow, they died so hard,
But gurgling dropped at last.
Their ghosts in gales repeat
Woe's us, Stone Fleet!

And all for naught. The waters pass —
Currents will have their way;
Nature is nobody's ally; 'tis well;
The harbor is bettered — will stay.
A failure, and complete,
Was your Old Stone Fleet.

The organization of the Stone Fleet was one of the strangest, counterproductive, and certainly one of the most useless strategies of the American Civil War. Simply put, it was the amazingly silly idea of blocking the harbors of Southern ports by sinking numerous ships in the harbor mouth.

Useless because ships sunk at the harbor entrance, although a temporary inconvenience, can be removed and counterproductive because it gave cause and motivation to the Confederates to savage the New England whaling fleets in delicious revenge against the pompous and self-righteous Quakers and Puritans of New England who participated in the insult.

Fortunately for the whales of the world, the decision was very productive. Not only were numerous whaling vessels intentionally destroyed by the Northern government, but the rage the decision caused to the South unleashed the Confederate raiders onto the whaling ships of New England in bitter retaliation.

Both the actions of the Union and the reaction of the Confederates proved to be most welcome news to the whales.

In April 1861, President Abraham Lincoln decided to initiate a naval blockade of Southern ports. The objective was to strangle commerce going into and out of the South, to stop the exports of cotton and tobacco to Europe and to prevent the import of armaments and food to the Confederacy.

The reasoning was sound, but in practice it was not a good idea. There were simply too many rivers, estuaries, bays, and harbors to effectively cover. In fact, merchants from Europe, especially Britain, seized the opportunity to make exceptional profits by sending blockade runners, and although some were caught, most made it through, primarily because the area patrolled was so vast and Union gunships were too slow and deep drafted to pursue blockade runners over the shallow bars and shoals. In fact, many blockade runners laughably joked that they guided their vessels into and out of Southern ports at night by the lights of the patrolling Union ships.

The idea to sink ships at the harbor entrance to Savannah and Charleston was first suggested by a Union naval officer named

Charles H. Davis. He immediately withdrew it after due consideration on the grounds that it was not practical. Naval engineers advised him that the soft, deep silt bottoms would simply shift and new channels would open around the wrecks.

But then the idea drifted into Washington, D.C., where Assistant Secretary of the Navy Gustavus V. Fox seized upon it and began to lobby for its implementation. Charles Davis did attempt to explain to Fox that although it was his idea initially, it was simply not a workable strategy. Fox ignored Davis, and as Davis observed, the idea became a "maggot" in Fox's mind and he would not let it go.

And thus, on October 17, 1861, the Secretary for the Navy Gideon Welles signed an order for the U.S. government to begin purchasing "as secretly as possible" old ships to be sunk at the entrance to Savannah and Charleston harbors.

It was also good business for one George D. Morgan of New York City who was granted the procurement contract for 2.5% of the cost of each old ship purchased. He was awarded the contract without the formality of submitting a bid. Of course, it helped that Gideon Welles had a sister married to a George D. Morgan of New York City.

Within weeks, Federal purchasing agents were scouring the docks of New Bedford, New London, Sag Harbor, Boston, Provincetown and virtually every seaport in New England, looking to buy as many hulks that he could find, for the more ships he could find and purchase, the more he would profit.

And what the agents found was a surplus of whalers.

It was a buyer's market in many ways because the Northern ship owners and insurers knew that their vessels would be at risk on the high seas for as long as the war continued.

In short order, four wharves in New Bedford became crowded with old whaling ships bought up by Ivory H. Bartlett and Sons. By November 1861, Bartlett had purchased twenty-five whalers, sixteen of them from New Bedford.

At first the whaling families of New Bedford thought that Bartlett was out of his mind, buying vessels, some of which were over half a century or more old. Rumors began to float that he was putting together a super whaling fleet, and the Quakers were amused because it was obvious that Bartlett did not know a thing about the whaling industry. But they were happy to sell them their old whaling ships nonetheless, and as one ship after another returned from the Pacific or Arctic voyages, they would be sold to Bartlett straight after the oil was unloaded.

The residents of New Bedford were even more surprised to watch the workmen strip the ships of harpoons, barrels, ropes, tackle and chronometers. Most of the canvas was removed and each ship was left with a single anchor. The crew quarters were ripped out and the insides opened up.

The "secret" was soon suspected when the workers began to drill holes in the hull and to insert lead pipes with flanges and that could mean only one thing. These vessels were being prepared for scuttling, and the most obvious reason for the scuttling of so many ships would be to blockade a harbor.

And this deduction was lent considerable weight as observers saw cartload after cartload of granite loaded into each ship in a very un-seamanlike manner, giving little mind to the distribution of weight in stowage.

On November 15th, the ships were moved to Buzzard's Bay.

The next step was for Bartlett to recruit a crew to deliver the ships, and there was an eager crowd of masters, mates and seamen hanging about, just returned from whaling and quite ready for a paid vacation and at the same time ready to do their patriotic duty for the Union, although officially they did not know the intent or the purpose of the ships filled with stone.

Politics was involved, for if an applicant was a Democrat, he was required to get the endorsement of a Republican to sign on.

What a sight it must have been, this great fleet of doomed ships filled with granite stone, sails tattered, hulls rotting, stripped of all comforts, leaking, the rigging moaning in the winter wind as a skeleton crew of Yankee sailors guided these great wooden corpses to their appointed resting places in the Southern harbors of Savanah and Charleston, each ship sinking fruitlessly in the churning mucky maw of the Ashley Cooper and Savannah rivers with no effective purpose.

My own experience at scuttling ships is considerable. I sank my own ship the *Sea Shepherd* in the harbor of Leixoes on December 29, 1979 to keep it from being seized after she was detained in the aftermath of our ramming and disabling the pirate whaler *Sierra* on July 16, 1979. Our crew then scuttled the *Sierra* on February 6, 1980 and two of the four Spanish whalers in Vigo harbor in April 1980. This was followed by the scuttling of half the Icelandic whaling fleet in November 1986, and the scuttling of numerous Norwegian whalers between 1992 and 2010.

I almost scuttled my ship the *Sea Shepherd II* in 1983 while blockading the harbor of St. John's, Newfoundland, to prevent the sealing fleet from leaving. In response to a threat to board my ship, I responded by declaring I would scuttle the *Sea Shepherd II* in the Narrows of the harbor of St. John's. The assault on my ship was called off, and our blockade was successful.

Another interesting comparison is that in 1972 when Greenpeace was founded there were two factions: the Quakers and Environmentalists. The Quakers were the Peace element and the Environmentalists were the Green faction. In 1975, the Quaker faction split from Greenpeace in protest to our anti-whaling campaign, which they fiercely and unsuccessfully opposed.

In the nineteenth century the Quakers were whalers; in the twentieth century the Quakers remained sympathizers to whaling.

In summation, the Great Stone Fleet was a colossal waste of time and money for the North. The entire operation was a failure, yet to the nation of whales it was a salvation. So many whaling ships that would never kill a whale again. It is my calculated opinion that this strategically useless campaign saved the lives of thousands of whales and contributed immensely to the survival of many species.

For this, the Union must be thanked and especially the obsession of Gustavus V. Fox, whose passion for the strategic folly turned out to have been a benefit for the whales.

CHAPTER V

Rebel Buccaneer

Captain John Newland Maffitt

It has been my experience that, when confronting overwhelming power, be it political, military, economic, or bureaucratic, the greatest weapon that can bring the confrontation to an even footing, or ultimately carry it on to victory, is individual passion.

My success for nearly four decades against illegal whaling, sealing, and fishing activities has been solely based on acting passionately, courageously, and with unpredictability, using a combination of deception, imagination, surprise, and audacity.

In no small part, I have been inspired by the Confederate captains who commanded the Confederate Naval Raiders, especially Raphael Semmes of the *CSS Sumter* and *CSS Alabama*, John Newland Maffitt of the *CSS Florida*, and James Iredell Waddell, of the *CSS Shenandoah*.

Of the three aforementioned Confederate captains, Semmes was the most notorious, successful, and the luckiest, Waddell was the most persistently stubborn, and Maffitt was without a doubt the most adventurous and the most courageous.

Over the years I have experienced campaigns that brought me to the same places as many of these Rebel vessels. My ships have slipped quietly out of harbors like Capetown, Nassau, San Juan, St. John's and Halifax. I have also run dark, hard pressed against the shore to avoid detection in the waters off Newfoundland, Costa Rica, South Africa, Australia, Iceland, and Norway. And I've played deadly chicken in head-to-head charges against warships from Spain, Norway, Denmark, the United States, Canada, and the Soviet Union, and the whaling ships accompanied by security ships from Japan.

I have felt the great joy of eluding capture and the even greater joy of sending whaling ships to the bottom. In recounting the adventures and the history of the Confederate raiders, I feel a deep kinship with these long dead sailors.

We pursued a common objective for different purposes, and we, as they, did so in the face of overwhelming opposition against much superior forces.

My experiences in fighting bureaucrats in ports around the world has clearly demonstrated that although a century and a half may separate our activities, the frustration and annoyance of having to deal with bureaucracies, manned by petty minded individuals, has not changed much.

Often when faced with such frustrations I turn to history for solutions, and it is amazing how solutions that worked for anti-whaling captains of the nineteenth century have also worked to make my own anti-whaling operations successful in the twentieth and twenty-first centuries.

The securing and outfitting of the *Florida* is an example of how courage and passion can carry a vision forward against what appears to be insurmountable obstacles.

In 1861 James Dunwoody Bullock had retained the services of F.S. Hull, one of the most prestigious of Liverpool's law firms. He needed to find loopholes in the British Foreign Enlistment Act, loopholes in laws that prevented British ship builders from outfitting warships for foreign powers. The law had not yet been tested, but the Liverpudlian lawyers believed they could defend the purchase and outfitting of a ship, regardless of intent, just so long as it was not outfitted to take on guns and ammunition.

Bullock was looking for cruisers that would utilize both steam and sail. He wanted wooden ships that could be easily repaired by carpenters. He needed large coal bunkers for distance.

By early July, Bulloch decided to contract the construction of a vessel to suit his needs, and to this purpose he engaged Miller and Sons of Liverpool. He selected a Royal Navy design for a fast dispatch gunboat and requested two significant changes. He wanted the hull lengthened to accommodate more coal, and he wanted to increase the amount of sail in order to increase the speed.

He named the vessel the *Oreto* and spread the story that it was being built for an Italian owner. Construction began immediately, and the building remained undetected by the U.S. agents until October.

Rumors reaching the ears of the U.S. Minister to Great Britain Charles Francis Adams resulted in a voiced concern that a Confederate warship was being constructed in a British yard.

Adams contacted the Italian embassy and discovered they knew nothing about an order for a gunboat. His suspicions were very much aroused when he discovered that the financing for the construction had been arranged by Fraser, Trenholm and Company, a firm Adams knew acted as bankers for the Confederacy.

The British investigated, but reported they could not find any evidence that the *Oreto* was being built for war or that she was connected to the Confederacy.

The U.S. could not prevent the *Oreto* from sailing on March 22, 1862, under the command of a British captain, James A. Duguid, and bound for Palermo, Italy, but they knew that there must be another vessel being prepared to transfer arms at another destination. Thomas H. Dudley suspected that the vessel aiding the *Oreto* was the *Bermuda* and ordered the U.S. Navy to shadow the *Bermuda* wherever she might go. Dudley, however, was mistaken. The arms were onboard the already departed *Bahama.*

After leaving Britain, the lone Confederate agent on the *Oreto* changed the captain's orders, forsaking Palermo and heading instead to Nassau in the Bahamas.

The agent was John Low. Bulloch had snatched him from Robert E. Lee's army and recruited him into the Confederate Navy as a master. He was well connected in Savannah, where his uncle ran a business, Andrew Low and Son, affiliated with two Liverpool trading firms, and a London headquartered insurance company. Low's job during the voyage was to recruit British sailors to remain on the crew of the *Oreto* after she would change registry to that of a Confederate raider.

Needless to say, this surprised many of the officers and crew who would either have to remain with the ship or depart in Nassau.

After a 37-day voyage, the *Oreto* arrived in Nassau and Low wrote a letter to Bulloch: "I took particular notice as regards the *Oreto's* speed under steam and canvas, and am happy to report most favorably of her in all respects... I now give you what I have seen her do during the passage: under steam, with smooth water, 10 ½ knots, and under canvas alone...13 ½ good."

Low also conveyed orders from Bulloch to turn the ship over to Lieutenant John Newland Maffitt when he arrived in Nassau.

Maffitt was enroute to the Bahamas on the Confederate blockade runner *Gordon*. He was one of the best blockade runners in the South, and for this reason Bulloch was of the opinion that Maffitt was the man to command the *Oreto.*

However, by the time Maffitt arrived, a week after the arrival of the *Oreto*, the ship was already embroiled in a bureaucratic and political squabble between the British authorities and the United States Consul Samuel Whiting at Nassau.

Whiting at first had thought the *Oreto* was just another blockade runner. He found out she was something else after an inspection by Captain Henry D. Hinckley of the HMS *Greyhound.* The British determined that the vessel had been built as a warship, but Hinckley reported to Whiting that despite his suspicions, without evidence of armaments, the ship could not be held.

Nonetheless, a U.S. task force of 12 Union warships entered the harbor led by the heavy cruiser USS *Cuyler*. There was no fooling the Union officers. What they saw was a warship, guns or not.

More trouble arose for the Confederates on May 3rd, when some twenty British sailors jumped ship from the *Oreto* and answered a call to the U.S. Consul in exchange for generous bribes. They testified that the *Oreto* was indeed brought to Nassau to be turned over to the

Confederacy as a warship. They also reported that Captain Duguid was a British master employed by the South in a deliberate attempt to disguise her identity.

As this drama was unfolding, the *Bahama* entered the harbor with the consignment of weapons and several known Confederate seamen from the *Sumter*. Low was able to quietly have the cargo transferred to a warehouse onshore.

Maffitt arrived on the 4th of May, discovered the problems, and was intrigued by the challenge. He happily took over the command from Low and proceeded to work on a plan to get the *Oreto* out of the harbor and the arms transferred.

And it was indeed a challenge. The *Oreto* was under twenty-four-hour surveillance by the Union Navy, and Union officers had her under continuous observation through binoculars. In addition, the very suspicious Captain McKillop of the HMS *Bulldog* was watching both the Union ships and the vessel they had under surveillance.

McKillop actually seized the *Oreto*, convinced she had taken arms onboard in the harbor. The Governor of the Bahamas, Charles J. Bayley, immediately countered that order and had the *Oreto* released. No guns had been found, although Bayley privately agreed with McKillop that there was justification for his suspicion. In response he increased the Custom inspections on all supplies going onboard the *Oreto*.

On June 5th, Captain Henry D. Hinckley returned to Nassau and relieved Captain McKillop. Hinckley then took it upon himself to seize the *Oreto* a second time because he also believed arms had been loaded, despite the Custom's watch.

This action angered the Governor and again he ordered the *Oreto* released. Hinckley attempted to disobey the Governor and threatened to move the *Oreto* to another port. This gave cause to the Governor to have his Attorney General intervene to pressure Captain Hinckley to follow the Governor's orders.

And into the midst of this squabble between the British politicians and the British Navy, with the U.S. Consul scurrying about to find evidence against the *Oreto*, and the Union Navy circling the vessel like cats around a trapped mouse, the vessel *Melita* arrived in the harbor with a cargo of supplies for the Confederates. Onboard were Captain Raphael Semmes, Lieutenant John M. Kell, and Surgeon Francis L. Galt, all from the crew of the notorious *Sumter.*

Semmes was on his way back to England, but his arrival ignited rumors that he would be assuming command of the *Oreto,* and this served Captain Maffitt nicely, allowing him to remain unknown and unsuspected.

Consul Whiting was able to force the Governor to seize the *Oreto* a third time. This time the *Oreto* was put on trial for violation of the Foreign Enlistment Act. However Whiting, believing he now had the Confederates stopped cold, made a mistake in sending a letter to Captain Hinckley praising him for forcing the Governor's hand. This caused the Governor to demand that Whiting be recalled for interfering with the business of the British government.

Despite this, Whiting was confident that the case against the *Oreto* would be upheld, and he was encouraged when he learned that Raphael Semmes had sailed on to England. He believed that this was evidence that the Confederates had already abandoned the *Oreto* knowing they would lose the ship. John Low had also returned to England. Only the British crew under Captain Duguid remained to defend the *Oreto* in court. Whiting did not have the slightest suspicion that Maffitt was still in Nassau pulling the strings for the South.

As the trial progressed, Maffitt demonstrated his expertise in espionage, spending funds to bribe police and witnesses. He bribed British merchants into testifying the *Oreto* was indeed a British merchant ship. Much to the U.S. Consul's annoyance and surprise, the ship was ordered released by the British court on August 7th.

Whiting immediately ordered the U.S. Navy to intercept the *Oreto* the moment it left port.

Maffitt, on the other hand, wasted no time in preparing the ship for sea. He did not have much of a crew. The British crew were paroled, and that left Maffitt with 7 Confederate officers who had been secretly living onshore and 14 deckhands, plus his own young stepson, J. Laurens Read.

As the *Oreto* was being readied for sea, the guns and ammunition were quietly loaded onto the vessel *Prince Albert* and ferried out to sea past the unsuspecting Union warships.

The USS *Cuyler* immediately observed that the *Oreto* was moving and began pursuit, but Maffitt took advantage of the neutral waters and anchored the *Oreto* close to the HMS *Petrel*. The *Culyer* began to circle the two ships until an irritated Captain Watson of the *Petrel* ordered the Union ship to return to the harbor or leave British waters. The *Culyer* retreated out to sea to await the *Oreto*'s departure.

The Union ships still were unaware that Maffitt was in command of the *Oreto* and Maffitt was the best damn blockade runner in the Southern States. As soon as the *Cuyler* withdrew, Maffitt set a course for Charleston. He saw the *Cuyler* take the same heading and then quickly came round Hog Island and dropped anchor in a cove, watching as the Union warship disappeared over the horizon in pursuit of where they thought he would be.

Maffitt then headed due South and met up with the *Prince Albert*. Both ships dropped anchor in Green Cay some sixty miles south of Nassau, where the guns were transferred. By August 16th, all the armaments and stores had been transferred.

On August 17, 1862, Captain Maffitt officially commissioned the vessel as the *CSS Florida,* and the Stars and Bars was hoisted up to the peak of the main mast.

The *Florida*, with many of her crew suffering from yellow fever, retreated to Cuba. But Maffitt had another problem. In the transfer of supplies, the rammers, sponges, and other necessities for manning the guns were not found.

With insufficient crew and guns that were essentially useless, Maffitt was facing some daunting challenges. But this was a man to whom challenges were welcome and who loved nothing better than to strive forward in the face of adversity.

The *Florida* under John Maffitt would soon outshine the *Sumter,* to become second only to the notorious *Alabama* under the command of Captain Raphael Semmes as the most feared raider of the Confederate Navy.

Having eluded the Union warships, Maffitt faced a more dangerous enemy upon reaching Cardenas, Cuba. Yellow fever struck him
and laid him low for a week. He grimly fought a painful death as
many of his crew died around him.

On August 29th, he regained consciousness in time to hear two
men discussing his condition. The two were Dr. R.H. Barrett of Georgia and another doctor from the Spanish warship, the *Guadalquivir*.
He overheard Barrett saying, "I doubt that the captain will survive
beyond noon."

The two men were quite startled when Maffitt spoke for the first
time in a week. "You're a liar, sir. I have too much to do. I haven't
time to die."

During that week he had lost six crew to yellow fever, including
his beloved stepson Laurens. Twelve new recruits arrived, and Dr.
Barrett resigned his post with the government hospital in Havana
and signed onto the *Florida* as assistant surgeon.

To make matters worse, the Union warships had tracked him
down again and were once more awaiting outside of a second harbor
for his departure. Short-handed and with his body still weak from
the fever, Maffitt did not hesitate to take on another challenge.

The *Florida* slipped out of the harbor when the Union warships mistook a Spanish mail steamer for the Confederate raider.
He hugged the dark coastline, arriving in Havana early the next
morning. So convinced were the Union sailors pursuing the Spanish vessel that was the *Florida*, they fired numerous shots as they
pursued. Fortunately for Spanish-American relations, all the shots
missed.

The Union warships regrouped and made way for Havana, effect-
ing a blockade of the harbor to await the departure once again of the
slippery Rebel raider.

Maffitt knew that the Spanish would only allow him to remain in
Havana until the sick onboard recovered. He also knew that because
of the sickness he would not find any recruits onshore, and the Spanish had refused him permission to purchase the supplies he needed
to man his guns.

Maffitt had his chair and himself carried up to the deck, where he made the decision to put to sea to break through the blockade and sail on to Mobile, Alabama. He knew it would be a highly risky operation and ordered his officers to prepare a fuse to destroy the ship should she fall into Yankee hands.

Captain Maffitt had developed blockade running into an art, and when the moon disappeared behind heavy clouds, he cut the cables and quietly got underway past Morro Castle, the Spanish fort that guarded the entrance to the harbor.

The Spaniards did not raise an alarm as the *Florida* swung close to the shore, using the land to shadow his outline from the Union vessels. He could see them but they could not see him, and within an hour, he was free at sea on a course for Mobile.

Not a single Yankee officer became aware that the *Florida* had disappeared from Havana until late the next morning. They had no idea where she could be heading and reported that she had simply vanished during the night.

Secretary Gideon Welles was furious. This elusive vessel was beginning to really irritate him. First the *Sumter* and now this. The *Florida* had not even experienced an engagement with another vessel, yet already she was a source of embarrassment to the Federal government.

I can readily identify with the crew of the Florida with regard to this escape. In 2005, our ship *Farley Mowat* was placed under arrest in Cape Town, South Africa. After four months of fruitless efforts to secure her release, and with her Canadian flag and registry stripped from her, we quietly slipped out of the harbor in the early hours of the morning in the wake of a large merchant vessel. The South African authorities were not aware of the escape until they read our media release much later in the day.

On September 4th, the *Florida* reappeared within sight of Fort Morgan, at the entrance of Mobile Bay. The problem was that between the harbor and the Raider were two Union gunships, the six-gun USS *Winona* and the 10-gun USS *Oneida.*

His officers advised him to wait until dark, but Maffitt was concerned that the deep draft of the **Florida** would make entering the main channel difficult, especially at night. He decided to run the blockade in the full light of day.

Without hesitation he made the dash, only to discover in short order that the approach was also being guarded by two additional Union warships, the two-gun schooner **Rachel Seaman** and the six-gun USS **Cayuga**.

With the four Union vessels closing in on his position, Semmes had his firemen shovel on more coal as he displayed all of his canvas in a mad sprint to run the blockade.

In command of the Union squadron was George H. Preble, who happened to be an old shipmate and close friend of Maffitt. They had forged a close friendship while serving together on the USS **Constitution**.

Such was the nature of this strange war that friends routinely found themselves trying to destroy each other.

Maffitt knew that the trio of Confederate forts guarding Mobile would limit the pursuit of the Union warships. He just had to get by the Union guns and into the shelter of the Southern firepower from the forts.

In his cabin, Commander Preble was completing his weekly report to Admiral David G. Farragut in Pensacola, Florida.

The deck watch at first thought the approaching vessel was the USS **Susquehanna**. A blockade runner boldly running towards them in the light of day was considered improbable.

But as the vessel drew closer, they could see from the thick black smoke that she was moving at her topmost speed, and that was suspicious.

Preble ran out to the deck and grabbed his glass. He made out the British ensign, and from her lines, there was no doubt it was an English gunboat. Her boldness, however, was unusual.

Preble held his fire but moved his ship to block the oncoming vessel.

Onboard the *Florida*, Maffitt had asked his officers to tie him to the quarter rail. He was feeling very weak, his body still recovering from the fever. He placed Quartermaster J.W. Billups and Boatswain Sharkey at the wheel. He trusted both men to stand their station even if the *Florida* were to be shot to pieces around them.

At fourteen knots the *Florida* headed straight for the *Oneida*, still flying the British colors. He was closing rapidly. Preble lost his nerve in the face of the oncoming ram and reversed his engines. The *Florida* held her course steady and passed within eighty feet of the *Oneida.*

Preble quickly maneuvered to fire a warning shot across the *Florida's* bow. At the same time the *Winona* and the *Rachel Seaman* stood off to port. They expected the *Oneida* to stop the British ship and were reluctant to get in the way.

The *Oneida* and the *Florida* came abeam, and Preble fired a second warning shot. When Maffitt refused to respond, the *Oneida* delivered a full broadside at point blank range, so close the two opposing crews could see the colors of each other's eyes.

The shots tore viciously through the *Florida,* smashing her boats, ripping her rigging, tearing her sails, and splintering the woodwork.

The *Florida* dashed forward, and as she did, Maffitt brought down the Red ensign and quickly hoisted the Stars and Bars. There was no doubt now that this was a Confederate warship. Preble ordered his guns reloaded and continued to pursue, along with the startled crews of the *Winona* and the *Rachel Seaman,* who had quickly manned their guns, sending shot after shot in the direction of the fleeing *Florida.*

Semmes did not have the ability to return fire. All he could do was shovel on more coal and attempt to replace the torn canvas in his bid to make the security of the forts, all the while as shots peppered the sea around him. With the Yankees targeting his sails and rigging, Maffitt ordered his men below, keeping only himself, his officers, and his two men at the helm above deck.

Maffitt later wrote of the experience saying, "The loud explosions, roar of shot and shell, crashing spars and rigging, mingled with the moans of our sick and wounded, only increased our determination to enter our destined harbor."

An eleven-inch shell smashed through the *Florida's* starboard hull only nine inches above the waterline, wounding nine men in the engine room and decapitating fireman John Duncan as he was feeding more coal into the fires. The shell carried on, tearing through the port side and exploding over the water. If the fuse had ignited the shell only a second earlier, the ship would have been utterly destroyed.

A shell from the *Winona* ripped through the ship's pantry and another tore the port gangway apart. The marines on the *Winona* sent volley after volley of rifle fire onto the decks of the *Florida,* with balls whistling past the ears of Captain Maffitt and the men at the wheel.

An officer on the *Oneida* later wrote, "Those who longed for his discomfiture could not but admire the steady bearing of the brave man who sat alone on the deck."

Slowly the *Florida* edged forward, gaining ground amid the hail of shot that lasted for nearly an hour, until finally she reached the protection of Fort Morgan's guns. Despite serious damage, nine men wounded, and one fatality, Maffitt delivered his ship into the arms of the Confederacy.

It was a terribly embarrassing incident for the North. With the Northern press screaming for Preble's head, Farragut ordered him dismissed from the Navy.

Arriving in the Mobile channel, Maffitt untied the rope that held him upright. He could barely stand, but he pulled himself to his feet and praised Billups and Sharkey for their courage in running the Yankee gauntlet.

As the *Florida* moved at half speed up the channel, a 21-gun salute boomed out from Fort Morgan and people gathered along the harbor front to cheer.

The *Florida* had been struck in 1,400 places, and torn and scarred as she was, she proudly dropped the hook victoriously off Melrose as the sun set over the bay.

There was no doubt it was one of the most courageous incidents of the war, certainly of the naval encounters.

Years later, Union Admiral David Dixon Porter, in his *Naval History,* expressed his open admiration for Maffitt. "During the whole war there was not a more exciting adventure than this escape of the *Florida* into Mobile Bay. The gallant manner in which it was conducted excited a great admiration even among the men who were responsible for permitting it. We do not suppose there was ever a case where a man, under all the attending circumstances, displayed more energy or more bravery."

The day after gaining safety in Mobile on September 12th, Lieutenant Stribling died of the yellow fever and the crew of the *Florida* were confined to the ship until the disease was arrested. The yellow quarantine flag finally came down on September 30th.

Repairs began on October 3rd, and the Union rushed more ships to guard the entrance of Mobile to prevent the *Florida* escaping. This had the benefit of weakening the blockade in other areas, allowing the runners to get through a little easier.

For four months the *Florida* lay at anchor in the bay, undergoing repairs while Maffitt recruited the crew he needed. Lieutenant Dulany A. Forrest reported on board on October 9th to replace the late Lieutenant Stribling. Lieutenant Samuel W. Averett arrived at the end of October. Maffitt, disappointed with Forrest, dismissed him and made Averett the Executive Officer. Maffitt took the opportunity to dismiss other crew he felt incompetent now that he had the pick of the Confederate officer corp to choose from. Maffitt requested and received Lieutenant Charles W. Read, a hero of the battle at New Orleans, and he also was pleased to sign on Lieutenant James L. Hoole, who had been wounded at Roanoke Island.

By January, the *Florida* had 19 officers and 116 men. This gave Maffitt a luxury not to be enjoyed by the other raiders: the *Georgia,* the *Alabama,* and the *Shenandoah.* The *Florida* crew were to a man all Southerners, and the majority of them were passionate Confederates.

But before the *Florida* could leave, Maffitt faced another obstacle. This one a bureaucratic one, when the Confederate Secretary of the Navy, Stephen Mallory, ordered that Maffitt be replaced by Lieutenant Joseph N. Barney. Mallory accused Maffitt of delaying his departure in Mobile so that he could enjoy the security and his celebrity on shore rather than face the perils at sea. Needless to say, Maffitt and his crew were angry at this insult, and Maffitt would have none of it. He went straight to Admiral Franklin Buchanan, the hero of the CSS *Virginia (Merrimack)* to appeal what he said was a grave injustice.

Buchanan agreed and sent off a letter to Mallory accusing the Secretary of meddling with his authority. He went further and appealed directly to President Jefferson Davis, who fortunately for Maffitt, was in Mobile at the time. The president telegraphed Mallory, and Maffitt had his command restored.

On January 11, 1862, the *Florida* was ready to return to sea, but whereas he had to contend with four Union ships coming into Mobile Bay, there were now thirteen blocking his way out. In addition to his old friend the *Oneida,* now under a different captain, he could see from the walls of Fort Morgan the 10-gun very fast USS *Cuyler,* and the very large 15-gun USS *Susquehanna*. It did not look good.

Maffitt needed an ally, and that ally would be found in nature. He needed the right night and the right conditions. On January 15th, he was given everything he needed when a violent northern squall erupted, with torrential rain and winds flinging the spray over the swells. At 02:00 hours, the *Florida* headed out of the bay and over the bar and made straight for the Union ships.

With three Union ships directly in front of him, Maffitt bore boldly down upon them. As the *Florida* edged closer, they quickly passed by the first vessel but were spotted by a lookout on the second. The call went out that a ship was attempting to head to sea. Maffitt did not waver but kept pushing forward, directly through the startled Union squadron. Ahead of him he could now clearly see the outlines of the *Susquehanna* and the *Cuyler* only 330 feet apart. They still had not seen him, but suddenly a flash of sparks from his funnel alerted the ships ahead and search lights blazed on, probing the darkness for movement.

The lights found the *Florida*, the entire Union squadron was alerted, and the Confederate raider sped on. The chase was underway.

Maffitt was worried only about the *Cuyler* and her superior speed. He left the others in his wake, but luckily the *Cuyler* was delayed getting off her anchorage and got off to a slow start. By morning the *Florida* was five miles ahead and the sea was rough, with a wind blowing from the Northwest. The *Cuyler* was faster, but not in such a sea, and slowly the Florida gained ground, only to see straight ahead another large Union warship, the *Brooklyn*.

Maffitt then made a very bold move. Instead of attempting to evade the *Brooklyn*, he maintained his course, bluffing his way past the heavy cruiser.

"The only evidence she gave of seeing us," Maffitt wrote later "was by showing a light over the starboard gangway, and continued gracefully on…taking us for one of their own gunboats."

Still the *Cuyler* pursued, until Maffitt deployed an old blockade runner's trick. He stopped his ship, shut down her engines, furled her sails, and allowed his ship to be obscured by the swells and sea spray. The *Cuyler* passed by and disappeared to the South.

I myself have used this tactic a few times. Once while being pursued by a Japanese security ship, I stopped the ship in amongst icebergs in a dense fog, shut down the engines and watched the Japanese vessel pass less than a mile away on our radar screen. Even with modern radar, in the right circumstances, it is still possible to lose a pursuing ship in this manner.

We also used a violent storm to slip past a Japanese security ship outside of Hobart, t donations.

The *Florida* was now finally free of pursuing Yankee warships and free to hunt Yankee commerce ships.

Washington was incensed! Gideon Welles and his entire navy were humiliated and ridiculed. The *New York Times* openly accused Welles of incompetence and the United States Navy of lacking the will to track down the Confederate raiders.

The *Times* also demanded to know why George Preble had been dismissed for letting the *Florida* into Mobile Bay, but there was no disciplinary action against the eleven captains who let the *Florida* out to sea again. Truthfully Welles was tempted to sack them all, but he simply could not afford to do so.

With every victim of the *Florida* from that day on until September 26, 1864, Welles was reminded of the cost of his navy letting John Newland Maffitt and the *Florida* escape to begin their reign of economic terror against Northern commerce.

Florida's Contribution

Although Captain John Maffitt was a courageous and successful Commerce Raider and the *Florida* an excellent ship for dispatching American merchant ships, both captain and ship did not make a significant contribution towards the diminishment of the Yankee whaling fleet.

The *Florida* did capture, bond and destroy a substantial number of merchant vessels but only took one whaler under Maffitt's command, the *Rienzi*. The *Florida* did take a second whaler, the 330-ton bark *Golconda* with 1800 barrels of whale oil, under the command of Captain Charles M. Morris.

Two whalers in total sunk.

On June 22, 1864, the *Florida* captured the whaling ship *V.H. Hill* of Providence. Maffitt described it as a poor prize and not worth burning so he bonded the vessel for $10,000 and unloaded his prisoners onto her decks.

On July 8th, the *Florida* had her one chance to engage a Union warship, the USS *Ericsson*, a Union ship under orders to search for the rebel ship *Tacony.*

The *Ericsson* was no match for the *Florida*. Her commander Joseph N. Miller retreated. The *Florida* fired a broadside with one shot striking the foretop. Fortunately for the *Ericsson*, a rolling fog moved in allowing the Union ship to escape.

Maffitt resumed his patrol catching the brig *W.B. Nash* straight out of New York City with a cargo of 650,000 pounds of lard. This made for a very energetic and bright blaze.

The fire was seen by the crew of the whaling schooner *Rienzi* of Provincetown. With the Confederate raider bearing down on them, the crew took to their boats, abandoning the schooner and her valuable cargo of whale oil to the Rebel torches.

The *Rienzi* had come so close to delivering the oil all the way from the Pacific. Within sight of the lights of Provincetown, the whaler burned small against the backdrop of the much larger lard-fueled fire on the *W.B. Nash*.

Chapter VI

Launching the Wolf of the Sea

The day that Captain Raphael Semmes, well on board the ship *Bahama* in the Azores, set eyes on the vessel known only as *290*, he said, "She was, indeed, a beautiful thing to look upon. Her model was of the most perfect symmetry, and she sat upon the water with the lightness and grace of a swan."

Semmes was delighted with what James Bulloch had delivered. It was not an easy task but there she was, ready for outfitting to transform her into what would be the deadliest commerce raider of the Civil War.

Standing on the bridge of the *Bahama*, Semmes said to his men, "Now my lads, there is a ship. She is as fine a vessel as ever floated."

The *Bahama* had delivered Bulloch and Semmes and his senior officers. The *Agrippina* had delivered the arms and the stores and the *290* had delivered itself to this rendezvous in the Azores.

Semmes organized a celebration on the quarterdeck of the *290* where he had placed bunting and flags and set a band to playing "Dixie."

As the unofficial anthem of the Confederacy stirred their hearts, the British flag was lowered and the Confederate ensign raised as Captain Semmes officially renamed the cruiser *the* CSS *Alabama.* It was August 24, 1862.

Securing the vessel for Semmes had involved a great deal of intrigue and espionage.

James Bulloch had commissioned the construction by the Laird Shipyard in Liverpool. No questions were asked.

It did not take long before the U.S. Consul to Britain, Thomas Dudley, became aware of the construction of the *290*, named for the fact that it was the 290th vessel built in the yard by Lairds.

Dudley put into motion a diplomatic and legal campaign to stop the ship and almost succeeded.

As this intrigue was taking place, Bulloch had bought an old sailing bark, the **Agrippina**. He loaded her with 350 tons of coal along with cannons, guns and supplies. There was no possibility of outfitting the *290* in Britain. The *290* was being constantly watched by Federal agents.

On July 26, 1862, Bulloch was contacted by a reliable but secret source within the British government and told that the *290* would be seized within 48 hours.

On Tuesday the 29th of July, Laird's took the *290* out for a sea trial. Two of the Laird brothers and two of their daughters were on the deck and it looked like a short festive excursion. Once away from the shore a small tugboat took the Laird family back to Liverpool and the *290* continued down the Mersey and into the Irish Sea, then headed north around the top of Ireland avoiding a Union warship guarding the south in St. George's Channel.

After rounding the top of Ireland, Captain Butcher, as instructed by Bullock, set course for the Azores. The order from London did arrive to stop the ship, but it arrived six hours after the ship departed.

Captain Semmes along with Bullock quietly boarded the steamer **Bahama** and departed unsuspected down the Mersey. At the same time the **Agrippina** departed without suspicion from London.

All three ships were bound nine hundred miles away to the island of Terceira in the Azores.

Captain Raphael Semmes at first glance was not an impressive figure of a warrior. He was 53 but looked older, below average height weighing no more than 130 pounds. What was impressive about him were his very determined grey eyes and a very well-groomed handlebar mustache.

What could not be disputed were his credentials as a formidable naval commander and his record of prizes taken while commanding the CSS *Sumter*.

As Bulloch left on the *Bahama* to return to Liverpool he watched the lights of the *Alabama* recede with mixed emotions. He had wanted to command the ship he had built himself. He was after all a sea captain.

But unfortunately for James Bulloch, he was too good at his job and the Confederacy needed him in England. He understood that and wrote, "Banishing every sentiment but hope, I predicted a glorious cruise for the dashing little craft and her gallant commander."

CHAPTER VII

Azorean Bonfires:
The Death of Nine Yankee Whalers

Ocmulgee, Ocean Rover, Alert,
Weather Gauge, Altamaha, B. Tucker,
Courser, Virginia and Elisha Dunbar

September 5th to 18th, 1862

R aphael Semmes now had the perfect ship for the task of hunting down Yankee merchant vessels. With the transfer of guns from the *Bahama* to the newly commissioned *Alabama* just outside the territorial limits of the Portuguese Azores, his now fully-equipped warship was sitting in the perfect location to avenge the New Bedford captains who had bottled up the harbor entrances of Charleston and Savannah.

He was in the right place at the right time, for it was the height of whaling season in the Azores. It was here that the whalers gathered to take advantage of the feeding and breeding waters of the Sperm, the whale that the whalers valued over all others; and where congregated the Sperm, so congregated the whalers.

However, things were different this year. For the first time ever in these waters, the whales now had an avenger in the shape of an ebony hulled 235-foot-long and 35-foot-wide cruiser.

The *Alabama* would become the most feared and successful of all the Confederate raiders, and her reign of terror against Northern commerce would begin with the wholesale destruction of Yankee whaling vessels in the waters off the Azores.

The whaling ship *Ocmulgee* was about to enter history as the first victim of the Confederate Raider *Alabama.*

The *Alabama* was sailing along on the eastern horizon when the lookout caught the flash of a white sail in the distance.

The *Alabama* gave chase. It was a lengthy pursuit. The brig was unusually fast and succeeded in escaping from the Confederate cruiser, although not without disappointment for Semmes and his crew. The pursuit brought them straight to the whaler *Ocmulgee,* her sails half raised and bobbing in the sea with the weight of a slain Sperm whale hanging from her side on tackles. The whalers were busily stripping blubber from the whale and the trypots were boiling with black smoke streaking into the sky.

The animal they had slain was a magnificent bull with a jaw that measured twenty-eight feet in length. He had put up a ferocious fight, but in the end had succumbed to the lethal harpoons, rifle bombs, and sharp lances. The sheer weight of the carcass had the *Ocmulgee* visibly listing.

The *Alabama* had found not just an ordinary whaler, for the *Ocmulgee* was considered one of the largest and most valuable ships in the entire New England whaling fleet. And as luck would have it, this whaler was ripe with provisions to fill the larder of the Confederate cruiser.

Captain Abraham Osborn was both master and part owner of the 454-ton ship out of Edgartown, Massachusetts. His face revealed both his astonishment and disappointment upon seeing the star-spangled banner lowered and the Stars and Bars raised. When he first saw the cruiser, he assumed she was one of the new warships that Secretary Gideon Welles had dispatched to protect the whaling fleets.

Captain Semmes would become fond of using the star-spangled banner as a lure to bring his victims within range of his guns, referring to the flag of the Union as that "flaunting lie."

Semmes appointed Lieutenant Richard F. Armstrong to board the whaler. Armstrong, wearing a gray uniform, approached the stunned whalers, and as he came alongside he loudly proclaimed, "You are a prize of the steamer *Alabama*." Armstrong returned to the *Alabama* with the Captain and the ship's papers, along with 37 prisoners. The crew of the *Alabama* then transferred what stores they could use, including numerous barrels of beef and pork.

Captain Osborn accepted his fate with the stoicism of a true sailor, although he did attempt to plea for the salvation of his ship and oil. Semmes looked at him and said, "You are my prize. I am going to burn the *Ocmulgee*, and every other vessel bearing the American flag I can catch. I will have the whole fleet of whalers."

As Captain Osborn stood on the deck of the *Alabama* with his wrists manacled in irons, he could only stare helplessly at his unmanned ship bobbing on the waves, awaiting the torch. So much oil, so much toil, all lost, and as if to underscore his loss, two whales brazenly surfaced alongside the *Ocmulgee* ship and slowly swam past the whale killer as if to mock him. Their tails rose out of the water as they sounded. The Yankee whale killer was not a happy man, nor would he be for some time, knowing that he would be returning home without a ship, without a cargo of oil, and with no hope for insurance because he was not insured for losses caused by a Confederate raider.

Semmes estimated the value of whale oil onboard at around $100,000 but delayed burning the ship until the next day. His concern was that the flames at night would alert other whaling ships in the area.

The next morning he put the *Ocmulgee* to the torch, and watched as the vessel became a funeral pyre for the remains of the Sperm whale carcass still alongside.

Arthur Sinclair wrote down the procedure for torching a ship when he described the destruction of the *Ocmulgee*:

"First you cut up with your broadaxe the cabin and forecastle bunks, generally of white pine lumber. You will find the

mattresses stuffed with straw, and in the cabin pantry part at least of a keg of butter and lard. Make a foundation of the splinters and straw, pour on top the lard and butter. One pile in cabin, the other in the forecastle. Get your men in the boats, all but the incendiaries, and at the given word – "Fire!" – shove off, and take it as the truth, that before you have reached your own ship, the blaze is licking the topsails of the doomed ship."

The decks of the *Ocmulgee* were so saturated with whale oil that Sinclair's meticulous preparations were much more than needed to quicken the flames of destruction.

With the whaler ablaze on the morning of September 6, 1862, Captain Semmes held muster on the Alabama.

Semmes wrote: "With clean, white decks, with the brass and iron work glittering like so many mirrors in the sun, and with the sails neatly trimmed and the Confederate flag at our peak, we spread our awnings and read the Articles of War to the crew. A great change had taken place in the appearance of the men…Their parti-coloured garments had been cast aside, and they were all neatly arrayed in duck frocks and trousers, well-polished shoes and straw hats."

After the muster, with the *Ocmulgee* smoldering in the background, Semmes placed all 37 prisoners with their personal belongings into three whale boats and gave them leave to row to nearby Flores Island. He also gave them bartering goods to make their stay with the native islanders more comfortable.

After landing on Flores, Osborn wrote to the U.S. Consul on Fayal to warn that the *Alabama* was preying on whaling ships off of the Azores and asked for help. Unfortunately, the closest U.S. warship was the USS *Tuscarora*, and she was sitting in the harbor of Cadiz standing guard over the long abandoned *Sumter*. There would be no help from the Portuguese. Even if they were inclined to assist, the few naval vessels that they had were back in Portugal celebrating the king's wedding.

However, before the whalers reached shore, the *Alabama* sighted the schooner *Starlight*. Semmes hoisted the British colors and gave chase. He fired his lee gun but the vessel did not respond nor did she hoist her colors. The *Alabama* fired a second warning shot and still the *Starlight* did not respond, forcing Semmes to fire a third shot that whistled through the air between the fore and main masts, only a few feet above the heads of the passengers on the deck.

That shot elicited a response as the American colors were quickly unfurled, and the schooner turned against the wind and came about to surrender.

Lieutenant Armstrong led his boarding party to the Starlight and delivered Captain Samuel H. Doane with his crew back to the *Alabama*.

Semmes had the eight prisoners clapped in irons but allowed the passengers the freedom of the cruiser. The next morning the passengers were taken to the Azores. As there were several females onboard, the Confederate officers, being gentlemen, personally escorted the ladies to the shore. Shortly after, Semmes had the crew brought to the island to join them.

He delayed firing the schooner, so as not to alert other vessels, and boarded a Portuguese whaling brig. After examining her papers, he released her with an apology, citing later that it was the only foreign vessel that he had ever stopped and boarded.

After releasing the Portuguese whaler, another whaler approached, safe in the understanding that the large cruiser flying the Union flag was a protector and a friend.

After capturing the schooner, Semmes brought down the Confederate flag and once again raised the Stars and Stripes. A passing Yankee whaler seeing the Union flags on both ships unsuspectedly approached the *Alabama* and her captive.

Third Officer James M. Wilson boarded the 313-ton *Ocean Rover* of New Bedford and brought her master and part owner James M. Clark of Plymouth onboard the *Alabama* to meet Captain Semmes.

Captain Clark was understandably upset. He was homeward bound after a 40-month cruise and had 1,100 barrels of oil when he decided to stop by the Azores to fill the few empty hogsheads he had left. His greed was his undoing.

Semmes paroled Clark and his crew into six whale boats, stuffed them with supplies and sent them off in the direction of the islands. The whalers could be heard singing as they rowed towards the distant islands, where they arrived safely at around 22:00 hours that evening.

The *Alabama* lay alongside the whaler and the schooner, waiting for morning to fire them both, when his 12-to-4 watch reported another sail after midnight just over a mile off, and bound for the islands.

The Confederate cruiser overtook the vessel at dawn after a four-hour chase and raised the British flag. When there was no response, Semmes fired a ball from his 32-pounder close enough to douse the crew of the fleeing ship with a cold shower of brine. Accepting defeat, the vessel came around into the wind and raised the star-spangled banner.

The *Alabama* responded by lowering the British flag and raising the Confederate ensign. Lieutenant Armstrong boarded the vessel and returned with Captain Charles E. Church. The vessel was the *Alert*, 16 days out of New London, and bound for a whaling station at Hurds Island in the South Indian Ocean, where she intended to hunt sea elephants for their oil.

The *Alert* was a famous former Indiaman and had the distinction of having Richard Henry Dana once serve upon her. As such, the vessel was immortalized in his memoir *Two Years Before the Mast*.

Armstrong removed her provisions, and placed Church and his crew into four whale boats loaded with supplies. He sent them to the islands, some fourteen miles off as their bark erupted in flames behind them, much to the benefit of thousands of sea elephants in the Southern Indian Ocean.

At the same time Semmes fired the **Starlight** and the **Ocean Rover,** sending forty months of hard dangerous work by the whalers, in the form of greasy black smoke, into the bright blue sky.

Semmes gave a very practical reason to the whaling captains for destroying their ships: "Every whale you strike will put money into the Federal treasury and strengthen the hands of your people to carry on the war. I am afraid I must burn your ship."

The rising smoke attracted yet another whaling schooner, the *Weathergauge*, six weeks out of Provincetown. Mistaking the rising smoke for the burning trypots of another whaler, Captain Samuel C. Small's curiosity was rewarded with seizure by the *Alabama's* crew.

The burning ships were like bait in a lobster pot, attracting one whaler after another into Semme's hands. His crew torched the *Weathergauge* and sent 15 more prisoners ashore to add to the rising population in the Azores.

And still the whalers kept arriving. On September 13th, the 119-ton hermaphrodite brig *Altamaha* was taken. She was five months out of New Bedford and her luck had been so bad that her captain, Rufus Gray, seemed to accept that the capture by the *Alabama* was just a natural extension of his long bout of ill fortune.

That very evening, the watch on the *Alabama* reported to Semmes that a large vessel was passing to windward. Taking up his glass, Semmes saw at once it was a whaler, some three miles off, and raised his sails to run her down. After a three-hour chase, the whaler stopped, and was boarded by master's mate George Fullam.

It was the 349-ton ship rigged whaling vessel *Benjamin Tucker*, with 340 barrels of whale oil onboard, and eight months out of New Bedford. Captain William Childs was surprisingly calm as he surrendered his ship.

Before the morning mist had evaporated, the watch on the *Alabama* spotted yet another whaling schooner on a course heading straight towards the Confederates. It too was quickly captured and turned out to be the 121-ton *Courser*, six months out of Provincetown.

The *Alabama* now had 68 new prisoners, all seated in eight captured whaling boats under tow. Semmes brought them within sight of Flores and cast them loose to make their way shoreward.

Semmes reflected on what the islanders could be thinking. "The traffic must now be considerable, in this little island, such was the avalanche of boats, harpoons, cordage, whales' teeth, whalebones, beef, pork, tobacco, soap, and jack knives that I have thrown on shore."

The captain of the *Courser* was a fine sailor and very much impressed Captain Semmes. He argued that he was not a supporter of the Union. Although Semmes liked the fellow, he was not to be dissuaded from his duty. The ship was from that den of Puritanism and Quakerism and he said, "There are too many white-cravatted, long-haired fellows, bawling from the New England pulpits, and too many house burners and pilferers inundating our Southern land, to permit me to be generous, and so I steeled my heart, as I had done on a former occasion, and executed the laws of war.

After letting the prisoners off, Semmes used the *Courser* for a bit of target practice, allowing the crew to fire three rounds from each gun at the schooner before setting her afire.

And still the bounty of unlucky whalers fell into his hands. On September 16th, the eighth nemesis of Leviathan to fall prey off the Azores was the 345-ton bark *Virginia*, only twenty days out from New Bedford.

Captain Shadrach R. Tilton thought his vessel the *Virginia* was fast for a whaler but lamented that she was no match for the *Alabama*. "It was like a rabbit trying to run away from a greyhound."

The *Virginia* was outward bound for the whaling grounds of the Pacific, and fortunately for the whales, she would never arrive in those distant waters. The recently departed vessel carried a bountiful supply of provisions, in addition to a large parcel of recent newspapers to bring the Confederates up to date on the progress of the war.

Semmes was also very much irritated and angry with the New England whalers, especially the New Bedford whalers, because of the New Bedford newspapers he seized from the captive whalers.

When Captain Tilton asked Semmes if it was necessary that he be placed in irons, a very annoyed Captain Semmes slammed down one of the New Bedford broadsheets he had in his hand and gave Tilton an angry stare. "You Northerners are destroying our property, and New Bedford people are having their war meetings, offering a $200 bounty for volunteers and sending out their stone fleets to block our harbors, and I am going to retaliate."

Tilton openly wept as all hopes of barrels filled with whale oil were extinguished, and the flames from the decks of the *Virginia* rose high, igniting the sheets and sending the bright glow of the flames for miles across the glassy seas.

On Thursday, September 18th, the seas began to roll and the sky darkened. The *Alabama,* flying the Union Jack, pursued yet another whaler. The bark *Elisha Dunbar*, a 257-ton whaler, three weeks out of New Bedford, raised the American flag only after she was fired upon.

Because of the deteriorating weather conditions, Captain Semmes sent two of his best boats under the command of Wilson. Of that decision he wrote, "I had a set of gallant and skillful young officers around me who would dare anything I told them to dare, and some capital seamen, and . . . maneuvering the ship, I thought the thing could be managed."

The boarding party was ordered to bring back only the ship's chronometer, her flag, and her crew, and to set the whaler on fire before returning.

The *Elisha Dunbar* was the only ship Semmes had destroyed without first examining her papers. There was, however, no doubt in his mind that the ship was a Yankee whaler.

Captain David R. Gifford had spoken with Captain Tilton of the *Virginia* only a few days before on September 11th. Now both ships were no more.

Semmes described the burning of the *Elisha Dunbar* in his journal:

"This burning ship was a beautiful spectacle, the scene being wild and picturesque beyond description. The black clouds were mustering their forces in fearful array. Already the heavens had been overcast. The thunder began to roll and crash, and the lightning to leap from cloud to cloud in a thousand eccentric lines. The sea was a tumult of rage, the winds howled, and floods of rain descended. Amid this turmoil of the elements, the Dunbar, all in flames, and with disordered gear and unfurled canvas, lay rolling and tossing upon the sea. Now an ignited sail would fly away from a yard and scud off before the gale; and now the yard itself, released from the control of its braces, would swing about wildly as in the madness of despair, and then the hull rocked to and fro for a while until it was filled with water and the fire nearly quenched, when it settled to the bottom of the great deep, a victim to the passions of man and the fury of the elements."

In just eleven days the *Alabama* had destroyed nine whaling ships and a merchant schooner, and in the process saved many thousands of whales from their deadly harpoons.

The whalers marooned temporarily in the Azores returned on passing ships to New England, where they embellished their experiences to the point of overly dramatic fiction. Although Semmes and his men had not harmed a single whaler, the rumors became exaggerated in the extreme. Tales developed and yarns formed of how Semmes had blown up one ship that resisted him, sending her to the bottom with all hands. They also highly exaggerated their treatment at the hands of the Confederates and overly assessed the value of their losses.

In some ways this helped the rebel cause, as the fictional accounts seeded fright and terror in the imaginations of the whalers and the merchantmen and contributed greatly to the decline in Northern shipping enterprises.

Chapter VIII

Confederate Corsairs

Lieutenant Charles W. Read T
The *Clarence* and the *Tacony*
1863

How could a small handful of Confederate sailors completely outmaneuver and make fools of the entire United States Navy?

The Union Navy had strength, tradition, honor, duty, discipline, guns, a bureaucracy, and of course a noble cause. Most importantly they had ships.

By contrast the Confederate Navy was vastly inferior: Never more than two cruisers deployed at any one time, the Southern ports blockaded, inferior weapons, very little organization, no tradition and most of the sailors not even from the Americas.

They were a ragtag, motley international crew, but they did have incredibly resourceful and extraordinarily brave officers who simply loved what they were doing. They loved the freedom, the adventure and the challenges, and they passionately loved their new nation, because their fledgling country was also the land where they were born, where their parents were born, and their parents before them.

At one point during the war, a captured young rebel soldier was asked by his Northern captors why he was fighting. He looked at them and without any hesitation answered, "Because you're down here."

If we look at the issue of slavery, there is no question that the South was wrong. Slavery was a great evil. The Northerners employed a more subtle form of slavery that lasted long after the emancipation. The young boys worked to death in the coal mines, the young women exhausted and sick laboring in the textile mills. Under wage slavery they were paid, and they were free in a manner of speaking, but they were in many cases more ruthlessly exploited than a plantation slave.

The Southern men and women, probably more so than the Northerners, understood tradition, honor, and loyalty and as they demonstrated in battle after battle they were more than willing to die for their cause just as the Northerners were willing to die for theirs. This titanic clash of passions was the reason that this war saw more casualties than any other American conflict. Family feuds are often the most bitter, and the most cruel.

But the one thing that most impressed me with the Southern officers who crewed the Confederate raiders was that although they were ready to lay down their lives for the Confederacy, they were not advocates of killing for their country. They destroyed commerce but they did not murder women, children, or even men. They were gracious to their captives and treated them well.

The men of the Confederate raiders fought a form of naval warfare that inspired me in my own efforts to fight illegal whaling, sealing, the slaughter of dolphins and the poaching of fish a hundred and twenty years later. They understood that the key to victory was to strike the enemy economically and not to take their lives. Theirs was a war against property, not life.

And although saving the lives of whales was not their intention, they were instrumental in the destruction of whaling as a major Yankee industry. As such these men were heroes and role models for myself, and more importantly they taught me much about maritime guerilla warfare. They also taught me chivalry, the importance of mercy, loyalty to a cause, and of course – honor.

To the merchants of the North and especially to the Quaker whalers of New England, the Confederate raiders were terrorists and pirates. U.S. Secretary of State William Seward did not win any favors with his foreign counterparts by constantly referring to the Confederates as pirates. In the eyes of Great Britain, Spain, France, Australia, and other nations, the Confederacy was a legitimate nation and these Confederate sailors were belligerents, but not pirates. But still, if truth be told, they had to have a pirate's devil-may-care, adventurous spirit to carry off some of their extraordinary deeds during their exploits upon the high seas.

The straightforward charge through the Union blockade was truly representative of this buccaneer spirit. John Newland Maffitt was not just any naval officer. He made up his own rules as he went along and those rules served him well.

After her dramatic escape from Mobile, the *Florida* captured and burned the *Estelle* off the coast of Cuba with her cargo of molasses and honey, bound for Boston from Santa Cruz.

As if to taunt the Yankees even further, he returned to Havana to take on coal and winter clothing. His smooth-talking diplomacy with the Spanish officials allowed him an in and out visit with little delay, enraging U.S. Consul Robert Schufeldt.

On the very day the *Florida* departed Havana, January 22nd, Maffitt intercepted two Yankee merchant vessels, the *Windward* bound for New York, and the *Corris Ann* out of Machias, Maine. He burned them both the same day.

Although Captain Maffitt was unaware of it, Captain Semmes and the *Alabama* were also hunting in the same waters and had passed within a hundred miles of each other. Only two weeks before, eleven days before the *Florida* had left Havana, the *Alabama* had sunk the Union gunboat USS *Hatteras*.

Welles and his navy were becoming very worried indeed. These two Confederate cruisers were not designed solely for preying on unarmed merchant vessels. They could put up a fight, as the *Alabama* had demonstrated with her victory over the *Hatteras.*

The *Florida* now had her guns in working order, with her gun crews now proficient with the two 7-inch Blakely rifles and the six 32-pounders. Her greatest asset, however, remained her speed.

The U.S. Navy was always just a few days behind the Southerners, but the two old sea-dogs Maffitt and Semmes eluded them at every turn through a strategy of unpredictability and a constant feed of misinformation that sent Union gunboats off in every direction but the right one.

Within a week of leaving Cuba, the *Florida* arrived back where she began, in Nassau, much to the annoyance of U.S. Consul Samuel Whiting, who was unable to prevent the cruiser from re-coaling. Maffitt had 26 seamen desert in the Bahamas, but he could afford to lose them and regarded their departure as an opportunity to get rid of the slackers and troublemakers. Their loss was partially offset by six others who illegally and quietly joined the crew the same day.

With his fresh supply of coal, Maffitt steamed down the channel and anchored so that Whiting could plainly see the ship. He waited until darkness and departed.

Secretary Welles almost had him that night. Rear Admiral Wilkes had by chance directed his ships to spread out and ordered the USS *Sonoma* to check out Nassau.

The *Sonoma* was approaching Nassau as the *Florida* was departing, and the Americans spotted her and gave chase.

Commander Thomas H. Stevens had the *Florida* in sight and the chase was on. Maffitt and his crew were perplexed by the way the *Sonoma* would almost catch up within the range of their guns and then would fall back. This happened three times as the chase lasted for 34 hours for over 300 miles until the *Florida* caught a more favorable wind, sending her over the horizon and out of sight.

The *Florida* was prepared to engage the *Sonoma* if the Union gunboat had closed within range, and being that they were both about equally matched in firepower, it was probably to the relief of both crews that the *Florida* escaped.

As for the mystery of why the *Sonoma* kept falling back, this was reported by Stevens back to Wilkes: "Three times we had the *Oreto* almost under our guns, when the blower belt parted and all that we had gained upon her was lost."

Maffitt headed towards New England, but a heavy gale near Cape Hatteras gave him cause to change his mind and he headed South instead.

On February 5th, the *Florida* was almost stopped once again when a large steamer could be seen approaching through dense fog, bearing directly down on them. It was the fast side-wheeler *Vanderbilt* fitted with eleven-inch guns. This ship had been donated to the Union Navy by the industrialist and financier Cornelius Vanderbilt.

The *Florida's* crew quickly cut their engines, and lowered the twin smoke stacks, hid the guns, and attempted to disguise themselves as a West Indies trader.

The huge warship slowed down and approached within hailing distance to take a closer look. After a few minutes, the *Vanderbilt* revved up her engines and disappeared speedily into the night, completely failing to identify one of the only two notorious Confederate ships in existence.

It was a close call. In his journal Maffitt wrote: "To have been rammed by this immense steamer would have closed our career, and we were rejoiced to see her leave."

It was certainly good news for the whales.

Even more embarrassing for the Union Navy was that the *Vanderbilt* was among the group of Union vessels with specific orders to hunt down and destroy the *Florida*.

And it was very bad news for the *Jacob Bell* on the last leg of her voyage from China to New York with a cargo of 1,380 tons of tea and 10,000 boxes of firecrackers. It was the most costly loss of any ship of the entire war. Her cargo was valued at $1.5 million.

The firecrackers added much to the spectacle of the burning clipper ship and the aroma drifting across the sea was of camphor and cassia. It gave a whole new meaning to the term gunpowder tea.

The *Jacob Bell* had been a beautiful ship. *Florida* midshipman Terry Sinclair wrote: "She rounded to – and as she lay thus with black hull, gilt streak, scraped and varnished masts, and snow white sails, there was a general expression of admiration coupled with regret that such a thing of beauty must be destroyed."

The *Florida* was low on coal and Maffitt was bound by a British rule that prohibited belligerents from bunkering more than once in a British port during a 90-day period. Lieutenant Baldwin on the *Vanderbilt* was certain that the *Florida* would bunker in a French port. He decided to head to Martinique. But Maffitt, making his own rules, headed to the British port of Bridgetown, in Barbados. With Southern charm he talked Governor James Walker into selling him coal, despite the fact that he had bunkered in Nassau only a month before. He left Barbados two days later with another ten new recruits. He also let it slip that he was headed towards Panama to waylay a treasure ship. The Union took the bait, and as they headed towards Panama he set a course for Brazil.

On March 6th he torched the 941-ton *Star of Peace* with 1,000 tons of saltpeter from India destined for the DuPont munitions work. Maffitt reported it as a "very beautiful fire" and was especially pleased to have deprived the North of valuable military supplies.

On March 13th the *Florida* captured the schooner *Aldebaran* out of New York, bound for Brazil with a cargo of flour, rum, wine, whiskey, brandy, and live lobsters in barrels of ice. Most of the alcohol went to feed the flames, as the 30-crew stood in irons on the *Florida's* deck.

On March 28th, the *Florida* captured the *Lapwing* out of Boston with a cargo of smokeless coal, furniture, and lumber. Maffitt transferred 10 tons of coal and decided to keep the *Lapwing* as a tender.

He gave Lieutenant Averett command of the *Lapwing,* along with three officers and 15 crew.

On March 30th, Maffitt captured and burned the *M.J. Colcord* out of New York and bound for Cape Town. As he was unloading goods from the ship, a Danish brig passed by and agreed to take all of his prisoners in exchange for part of the cargo.

On April 16th, the *Florida* overhauled, captured, and burned the 1,300-ton clipper ship *Commonwealth of New York* and bound for Boston with a cargo worth $370,000.

The *Florida* had arranged to rendezvous with the *Lapwing* at Fernando de Noronha, off the coast of Brazil.

In 2002, I took my ship *Ocean Warrior* down the coast of South America from Trinidad and Tobago to Fernando de Noronha searching for illegal drift netters. We stopped at the island and arranged to do joint patrols with the Brazilian Ministry of Conservation. We spent a month patrolling with Brazilian rangers, and they were very interested in the stories that I told them of the Confederate raiders and their operations in the same waters.

Fernando de Noronha is an exceptionally beautiful island with a very notable landmark, a 200-foot-high tower of solid granite pointed at an angle towards the sea. It was a penal colony during the Civil War, but when we visited it was considered one of the most favorite tourist destinations by wealthy Brazilians. It kept the poorer visitors away by having very expensive prices for most nearly everything. But the people were just as friendly to us as Maffitt reported they were to him.

On April 23rd, the Florida captured the *Henrietta* out of Baltimore bound for Rio de Janeiro, with a cargo of 3,250 barrels of flour, 600 kegs of lard, and thousands of candles.

The master of the *Henrietta,* George Brown, was a Southern sympathizer and Maffitt took quite a liking to the man. Not enough to save his ship, but Brown took it all in stride. As his ship brilliantly burned, fed by the lard and spermaceti candles, George commented: "Doesn't she burn pretty? She belongs to Mr. Whiridge. He is a great Union man."

The next day, the *Florida* captured the clipper ship *Oneida,* out from Shanghai with tea and silk. The cargo was valued at one million dollars. Maffitt gave each of his crew two bolts of silk and joked that they were well supplied with tea for the duration of their voyage. The famous China clipper erupted in flames two hours after her capture.

On May 6th, the coffee drinkers on the *Florida* were rewarded with the capture of the brig *Clarence,* bound for Baltimore with 10,000 bushel bags of coffee. Maffitt offloaded 300 bags when he was approached by Lieutenant Charles W. Read, with a request to not burn the *Clarence,* but to turn it over to him so that he might convert her to a raider.

Whereas Maffitt was exceptionally daring, he was also practical and had a sober grasp of reality. He took calculated risks.

Maffitt wrote of his young lieutenant when he first joined the crew in Mobile, "Mr. Read is quiet and slow, and not much of a military officer of the deck, but I think him reliable and sure, though slow."

Two months later Maffitt reported in his journal that Read "was daring beyond the point of martial prudence."

One thing for sure is that Read was a man who hungered for action. He had graduated in 1860 from the U.S. Naval Academy but served only seven months before resigning to volunteer for service in his home state of Mississippi. At the battle of New Orleans, he had been in command of the beleaguered *McRae* after his captain had been fatally wounded. He fought the Yankees until the *McRae* was destroyed, and then took over the command of the grounded *CSS Resolute,* which had been abandoned by another Confederate commander, and continued to fight the enemy. Cited for bravery he was assigned as a gunnery officer to the ironclad *Arkansas,* where he stood his ground in the face of Admiral Farragut's far superior fleet at Vicksburg.

Looking at the *Clarence*, Read requested permission of Maffitt to take the newly captured vessel and with 20 men from the *Florida*, he offered to sail straight into Hampton Roads and attack the Union ships in their own port.

With her consignment of coffee and her papers in order, Read was certain he could pass through the blockade without interference from the Union Navy. He would then commandeer a steamer and break back out through Union lines to rejoin Maffitt at sea.

Maffitt was intrigued and thought the plan was worth trying. He once proposed to Mallory to do the much the same thing, to raid and burn the New York Navy Yard. Mallory had rejected the plan as too risky. Mallory was not in a position to reject or approve this plan. Maffitt was, and he gave Read his blessing.

In addition to the *Clarence*, Maffitt gave Read a brass six-pounder Howitzer and ammunition and said, "You'll be on your own, no orders to hamper you. Your success will depend upon yourself and your sturdy heart."

The new Confederate raider *Clarence* was commissioned on May 7, 1863. Read was 23 years old.

The *Clarence* moved north towards the coast of America. In addition to his Howitzer, Read had built a battery of Quaker guns: Wooden cannons on wooden gun carriages all painted black with gun ports cut into the sides to run them out.

The fake guns served him well. On June 6th, 250 miles west of Bermuda, the *Clarence* captured the bark *Whistling Wind* out of Philadelphia. Her cargo was coal bound for the Union squadron on the Mississippi. Read took great pleasure in burning that cargo after he discovered the intended destination.

On June 9th the *Clarence* captured and burned the Boston bark *Mary Alvina,* bound for New Orleans with supplies for the U.S. Army. From newspapers on the *Mary Alvina* he discovered that the navy's increased security for all ships entering U.S. ports would present obstacles he knew he could not pass. He decided to forego his ambitious plans to attack Hampton Road and headed north towards New England to inflict what damage he could. He was also not happy with the *Clarence,* and he needed a ship that could more legitimately pass through the Union lines.

On June 12th Read captured the bark *Tacony.* He decided that the newly captured ship would serve him better and made preparations to transfer his six-pounder over to the *Tacony.* As he was doing so, the Yankee schooner *M.A. Schlinder* approached. Without hesitation, Read captured her also, and set her on fire.

The captain of the *Tacony* was put onboard the schooner *Kate Stewart* along with Read's other prisoners. He had captured the *Kate Stewart* the same day but decided to bond her because of twenty female passengers onboard bound for Mexico. Before releasing the prisoners, Read told them that a large Confederate armada was moving towards the Atlantic coast.

The *Clarence* was abandoned, her short career as a Confederate raider ended when Read put the torch to her. As they sailed away, the aroma of 8,000 bags of coffee still in the hold of the doomed ship drifted towards them.

Read had prearranged a rendezvous with the *Florida* in the event that the Hampton Road plan could not be carried out. He headed north to meet up with the *Florida* unaware that Maffitt had been delayed for fifteen days in the Caribbean waiting for the *Lapwing*.

Read's little tale of the Confederate armada caused a major panic all along the Atlantic coast with rumors that both the *Florida* and the *Alabama* were part of the large Confederate fleet and that an attack was imminent.

The Union dispatched 38 warships to patrol the coast to search out and destroy the rebel pirates. Despite this the *Tacony* was not discovered as the navy scoured the seas for the *Clarence*, completely unaware that the *Clarence* was no more.

On June 15th, the *Tacony* captured the brig *Umpire* some 300 miles off the mouth of the Delaware River.

That same evening a Union naval vessel passed close by the *Tacony*. Read hid his prisoners below the deck. A Union officer hailed him saying they were in search of the pirate vessel *Tacony*. Read picked up the trumpet and responded, "Yes we saw her at dusk chasing an East Indianman." He gave a false heading and was relieved to see the Yankee warship steam away on the false trail.

The next morning a second U.S. Navy vessel hailed the *Tacony*. Once again he misled them and sent them off in pursuit of a bogus ship.

On June 20th, Read captured the large passenger vessel *Isaac Webb*. He could not destroy her with 750 passengers onboard so he bonded the vessel. As he was returning to the *Tacony*, a fishing vessel called the *Micabar* approached to see if the larger ship was in trouble, seeing that both vessels he spotted were stopped. Read poked three of his Quaker guns out through the port, captured her in full view of the passengers and put her to the torch.

The next day the *Tacony* captured the clipper ship *Byzantium* with a cargo of coal from Newcastle bound for New York. The *Byzantium* went up in flames. That same day on June 21st, Read overtook the bark *Goodspeed* bound for New York in ballast. She also was put to the torch.

Both the *Goodspeed* and the *Byzantium* had passed Union naval vessels that very day. The press was outraged that this small Confederate raider could inflict so much damage right under the noses of the United States Navy.

A day later, on June 22nd, the *Tacony* captured five New England fishing vessels and burnt four of them, placing seventy-five prisoners onto the fifth to be transported to shore.

Continuing north, Read captured and burned two more fishing schooners, the *Ada* and the *Wanderer.*

On the 24th he captured the large clipper ship *Shatemuc* bound from Ireland to New York with hundreds of immigrants. The ship carried tons of war supplies for the Union but Read decided that he could not kill the passengers and reluctantly set her free. Later in the day he captured the fishing schooner *Archer*.

By now the U.S. Navy had a very accurate description of the *Tacony*. Read decided it was time to change ships again and commandeered the *Archer,* putting the *Tacony* to the torch.

The 38 Union ships continued to search for a ship that was now no more, little suspecting that the new Confederate raider was now a fishing schooner.

Lieutenant Read was a natural tactician and a very elusive chameleon. He was also thoroughly enjoying himself, as were his men.

Read commissioned the *Archer* partially in jest as a new Confederate man-o-war and raised the Stars and Bars.

The morning of June 26th found the *Archer* laying just off of Portland, Maine. Read invited two lobstermen who were fishing from a dory onboard for breakfast. The lobstermen gave him a full description of the defenses of Portland harbor. The Confederates were especially interested to hear that the United States Revenue cutter *Caleb Cushing* was in the harbor. This ship was a schooner-rigged vessel with two guns, a 12-pounder and a 32-pounder. He also learned that a large passenger liner, the *Chesapeake,* was at the wharf and preparing to sail for New York City. He then informed the two aston-ished fishermen that they were now prisoners of the Confederacy.

Read had the lobstermen pilot them into the harbor and then placed them in irons below deck. The plan was to capture the *Chesa-peake,* but his engineer reported that he would not be able to handle the machinery on the larger vessel by himself.

Disappointed but not undaunted, Read decided to capture the *Caleb Cushing* instead.

It was an opportune time. Most of the crew were onshore for the night. They would be returning in the morning to put to sea. Their mission was to hunt down the *Tacony.* Little could they imagine that the crew of the *Tacony* were quietly rowing into the harbor and up to the side of the revenue cutter.

The Confederates boarded the *Caleb Cushing* quietly and with-out a shot fired, had the entire crew, including the ship's ranking officer Lieutenant Dudley Davenport, in irons.

Unfortunately the wind and tide turned against Read. Unable to make sail, he had his men row back out of the harbor towing the rev-enue cutter past the guns of Fort Preble that were guarding the bay.

The morning found them five miles outside of Portland, safely beyond the guns. Read called in the boats and served breakfast, invit-ing his old Annapolis classmate Lieutenant Davenport to the table. Being that Davenport was a Southerner, Read jokingly teased him for choosing the wrong side in the war.

Read then announced that the *Caleb Cushing* was his latest flagship.

Onshore the news quickly spread that the *Caleb Cushing* had mysteriously disappeared. Suspicion immediately fell on Davenport the Southerner, with accusations that he had stolen the ship.

Mainers have a tendency to act, and act they did. Without any authority the Port Captain Jedediah Jewett commandeered the Bos-ton sidewheel steamer *Forest City,* enlisted the crew of the revenue cutter that had spent the night on shore, and 36 men from Fort Pre-ble. He brought two 12-pounders onboard and by midmorning was underway, followed shortly thereafter by the faster *Chesapeake,* drafted into action by Portland's mayor Jacob McLellan. He brought on a detachment of the 7th Maine volunteers and 20 volunteer citizens armed with old rifles and rusty swords. Following these two vessels were dozens of Portland citizens in anything that would float all anxious for a front row seat for the action.

As the *Forest City* came within range, Read sobered them quite quickly with a shot from the *Caleb Cushing's* 32-pounder. The shell fell some fifty yards off the bow. Three more shots on each side made Jewett fully aware that Read could hit them if he so desired.

However in a rash move, Jewett and Mayor McLellan decided to charge the Confederates and ram them with both the *Forest City* and the *Chesapeake Bay*. It would have been a disastrous move for the Mainers if not for the fact that Read had run out of ammunition and Davenport refused to divulge where the reserve ammunition was stored.

Read had plenty of gunpowder but he could not find any shot. He fired a barrage of cutlery and crockery but he could plainly see that he could not outrun his pursuers and he had nothing of substance to stop them with.

He was not without a sense of humor, however. He loaded a ball of Dutch cheese into the 3-pounder and scored a direct hit across the deck of the *Chesapeake* and her very surprised crew.

Read then ordered the cutter destroyed and for the crew to abandon ship. The *Caleb Cushing* became the 22nd prize in 21 days for the little group of Confederate raiders. The *Archer* was quickly captured and Read and his men were brought back as prisoners to Portland.

The citizens of Portland accomplished what 38 Union warships had not been able to do – bring the rebels to heel. But the rebels under Read had demonstrated what a small passionate band of men could do, armed with imagination and courage. One ship, five barks, nine schooners, 1 brig, and a government cutter destroyed by rebel fire.

Lieutenant Read and his men had not sunk any whalers, although they certainly put some fear into the Quaker whalers of Massachusetts, and kept a few of them bottled up in port for some time.

Read and his men illustrated even more than Maffitt that seemingly impossible tasks can be taken on and victories won through sheer audacity, fired by courage and passion.

For myself I am well acquainted with Portland, Maine, having brought my own ships into Casco Bay in 1983 and again in 1998. I recruited quite a few volunteers there and I can certainly see how the citizens of Maine had the gumption to take matters into their own hands. I myself was raised on the Canadian side of the Maine/New Brunswick border just across from Eastport, and that practically makes me a Mainer myself.

It was a pleasure to relate the story of Lieutenant Read and his small band of rebel sailors to my crew during our two visits, the story of Lieutenant Read and his small band of rebel sailors and how their 21 days of raiding on the Eastern seaboard had taken 22 prizes, always a few steps ahead of the Union navy, changing ships three times, and eluding 38 warships occupied solely with the task of hunting them down, a task for which they failed miserably.

I did appreciate that Read fired a ball of Dutch cheese at his pursuers. The fact that he scored a direct hit where his lethal shots missed indicates to me that he was not inclined to take lives unless absolutely necessary, and in this case he could see there was no escape. His men were quite proficient with artillery and although the claim is that he could not locate the reserve ammunition, I find that hard to believe.

Confederate raiders throughout the war did not kill civilians and they were very reluctant to kill U.S. Naval officers. As Read and Davenport demonstrated, they were more likely to sit down and have breakfast together. There was rivalry, but not hatred. They had gone to the same schools, served in the same navy, and had been guests in each other's homes.

Since I began my campaigns to defend whales and life in the ocean I have also not injured a single person. My objective has been like the Confederate raiders, to inflict economic damage on my opponents.

To this end I have tossed stink bombs and used water cannons and paint guns but never anything designed to cause injury. I also tried where I could to inject humor into our tactics.

During one exchange with the Japanese whalers we fired crocodile eggs onto the deck of the Japanese factory ship *Nisshin Maru*. Not real crocodile eggs but novelty eggs from the Australian Zoo. When they landed on the deck, as soon as they became wet, they broke open with expanding foam crocodiles. The look on the faces of the whalers was priceless.

Lieutenant Charles Read and his men were imprisoned at Fort Warren in Boston and released a year later during an exchange of prisoners. He returned to fight the Union during the final days of the war, but not onboard a raider. By then the Confederate war at sea was nearly ended, except for the *Shenandoah*.

CHAPTER IX

The Final Defiance of the *Alabama*

The Battle between the
USS *Kearsarge* and the
CSS *Alabama* Cherbourg, France
June 1864

Onboard the USS *Raritan* in 1846, two United States Naval officers shared a common stateroom. They were good friends and both shared the fact that each had lost a ship under their command prior to being assigned to the *Raritan*.

Their friendship, however, went back even further to when they both served together onboard the USS *Cumberland* as midshipmen during the Mexican War. They had both received their first commands at the same time.

John Ancrum Winslow of Wilmington, North Carolina, was given the command of a small vessel captured from the Mexicans that had been renamed the *Morris*. Raphael Semmes had been given command of the brig *Somers*.

Winslow lost the *Morris* on a reef outside of Tampico.

About the same time the *Somers* capsized during a sudden and violent storm and Semmes narrowly escaped with his life with many of his crew lost.

These two men who rose through the ranks together with similar records of advancement and misfortunes were destined to meet one another on opposing sides eighteen years after they joked and shared meals together on the *Raritan*.

When the war began, Winslow had elected to stay with the Union although he was born a Southerner. Semmes resigned from the U.S. Navy to join the Confederate Navy.

In 1862, Union Secretary of the Navy Gideon Welles sent Captain Winslow to the Azores to take command of the 1,031 ton sloop-of-war *Kearsarge*. The ship took her name from a rock of the same name that stood as a landmark in New Hampshire.

Winslow was not happy with that decision. He felt his seniority, experience and abilities qualified him for a better command instead of this third-rate man-of-war normally skippered by a mere lieutenant commander.

He was a touch envious of his former friend's illustrious reputation as the Confederate "Wolf of the Sea."

He was also disappointed to find that upon reaching the Azores the *Kearsarge* was to be dry-docked in Cadiz, Spain, for the next three and a half months. The delay, however, had the benefit of allowing him to recover from chronic malaria and an infected eye.

His deep-seated sense of duty and his naturally stubborn and stoic nature pulled him through his illness and by the time the *Kearsarge* was ready to sail, he had recovered enough to assume command.

The *Kearsarge* had already spent more than two years in a fruitless search for the elusive Confederate commerce raiders. Although constantly patrolling the English Channel, the Bay of Biscay and the Mediterranean, the *Nashville*, the *Florida* and the *Georgia* had all evaded the *Kearsarge*.

Winslow felt that his search for the *Alabama* would also prove to be as frustratingly fruitless. For over a year he searched for the vessel commanded by his old friend and shipmate Raphael Semmes. He chased after every rumor and every shred of intelligence provided by the network of Union spies operating across Europe. Almost all of them led to dead ends. The *Alabama* was a phantom to the Union, constantly striking and disappearing.

But then a telegram reached Winslow as he was lying at anchor off Flushing in the Netherlands. The United States Ambassador to France William L. Dayton had sent the telegram from Paris to inform Winslow that the *Alabama* had just anchored in the harbor of Cherbourg.

An excited Captain Winslow assembled his crew on deck and announced, "Men, I congratulate you in saying that the *Alabama* has arrived in Cherbourg, and the *Kearsarge*, having a good name in France and England, is to have her cruising ground off that port."

The *Kearsarge* weighed anchor and set off down the channel for Cherbourg, her crew eager to do battle with the *Alabama*.

On the morning of June 14, 1864, the *Kearsarge* reached Cherbourg and took up a position outside of the harbor. Upon seeing her arrival, Semmes realized that he was in a difficult position. The *Alabama* desperately needed repairs, their powder was decaying and his men were exhausted. He knew he could not slip easily past the *Kearsarge* and if he delayed, other Union ships would arrive to bottle him in for the duration of the war. He could not legally enlist new crew or take on munitions in France and he was no longer welcome in England or Spain.

Semmes realized that the moment had arrived when he would have to engage in a full-out sea battle. He smiled at the irony of having to confront Winslow. He respected the man and knew him to be courageous and determined. He also still considered him a friend.

Not since the War of 1812 had a United States warship engaged in battle with another warship. This would be no skirmish but a full-blown classic sea battle and both Semmes and Winslow were not only ready for it, they both seemed energized by the prospect. They were both career naval officers and they could both see the historical significance of what was fast evolving into a showdown between the two of them and their respective ships and crew.

That engagement in 1812 had taken place just outside of Boston harbor when Captain Philip Broke in command of the British frigate *Shannon* challenged Captain James Lawrence of the American frigate *Chesapeake* to "meet and try the fortunes of our respective flags."

Although the *Alabama* was in ill repair, Semmes had longer-range guns and his ship was faster although he was uncertain as to how much the growth on her hull would slow her down. His major advantage was the courage and skills of his officers and the weathered experience of his men.

Most of the *Alabama's* crew were English and owed no allegiance to the South but they were all men of duty, loyal to their legendary captain and his ship and all were eager to match their abilities against the arrogant Yankees.

A northern Yankee crew commanded by a Southern captain against an English crew commanded by Southern officers off the coast of France to be fought before an audience of thousands of European spectators. Both ships under the commands of skippers who had been mutual friends and shipmates for many years. Such were the strange circumstances of this Civil War.

A century and a half later I found myself in a similar situation with my own ships in conflict with the Japanese whaling fleet. My ships flew the flags of the Netherlands and Australia with officers and crews from some thirty nations. Like the Confederate raiders, Sea Shepherd ships depended upon multinational crews loyal to the mission, the ships and their captains.

Semmes was resigned to this battle to the point of willfully ignoring concerns brought to his attention by his officers. He was fully aware that the copper sheathing on his hull was damaged and that many of the shells in his magazine were defective. He was also very much aware that the *Kearsarge* could throw 430 pounds of metal to his ability to fire 360 pounds. Additionally it had been brought to his attention that the *Kearsarge* had been armored with chain. Semmes would later insist that he knew nothing of the chains, yet it was common knowledge that the *Kearsarge* had 120 fathoms of chain behind one-inch pine planking protecting her midship hull section.

It was as if, with his resignation to fight, Semmes simply dismissed the disadvantages to the *Alabama* and steeled himself to carry the fight through to victory by the strength and power of his own will and his faith in the passion of his crew.

I can fully appreciate both his position and his resolve. My entire career has been one of confrontation against foes with faster, stronger, and more powerful ships. We have taken on, endured

and survived engagements with ships armed with guns whereas we carried no guns at all. Through all these engagements I myself put my trust and my faith in the passion and courage of my crew of international volunteers.

Semmes would not surrender without a fight. It was not in his nature and no matter the risks, he was ready to do battle with his old friend Captain Winslow.

Semmes sent a note to Samuel Barron, the commander of the Confederate Navy in Europe. He sent a copy of the same note to the United States Consul in France. He wrote the same message in his journal:

> "My crew seem to be in the right spirit, a quiet spirit of determination pervading both officers and men. The combat will no doubt be contested and obstinate, but the two ships are so equally matched that I do not feel at liberty to decline it. God defend the right — and have mercy upon our souls of those who fall, as many of us must."

Semmes was ill and he was cornered, but he firmly believed he would win the day.

"I will fight on Sunday. It has always been my lucky day," he said.

Semmes sent a message to Captain Winslow through his agent and the U.S. Consul, "My intention is to fight the *Kearsarge* as soon as I can make the necessary arrangements. I hope they will not detain me more than until tomorrow evening, or after the morrow morning at furthest. I beg she will not depart before I am ready to go out."

In preparation for the fight, Semmes transferred 4,700 British gold sovereigns along with the payroll records, the ransom bonds of captured vessels he had released and the chronometers of his prizes to Confederate agents. This was a prudent and practical precaution but Semmes was not being defeatist. He retained the flags of the captured vessels, over a hundred of them plus the sword that had been surrendered to him by the captain of the USS *Hatteras*. He kept his journal onboard. He did not write a farewell letter nor did he leave a will. He intended to win the day and stated that he would "prove to the world that his ship was not a privateer, intended only for attack upon merchant vessels, but a true man-of-war."

A mild westerly breeze accompanied the rising sun as crowds began to gather along the shorefront of Cherbourg. Some artists set up their easels, among them, allegedly Edouard Manet. There is some dispute as to if the famous artist was in fact among the crowd but he did later unveil a beautiful canvas in his unique Impressionist style of the *Alabama* sinking solemnly and heroically within a whirlpool. Some people waved American flags and others waved Confederate flags. It was a bright Sunday morning and by 09:00 hours some fifteen hundred people had gathered. Never before in history had a naval battle taken place before such a crowd of spectators.

The cooks on the *Alabama* prepared a hearty breakfast and the crew were in a very upbeat mood as they ate.

At 09:45 hours, the French ironclad *Couronne* escorted the *Alabama* to the western entrance of the harbor. In their wake at a safe and respectful distance came a small contingent of yachts. One of them was the *Deerhound*, owned by a wealthy Englishman and Confederate sympathizer named John Lancaster. On board were his wife, niece, a nurse and three sons. Earlier that morning they took a vote on whether to sail out to see the battle or to go to church. The vote was a tie until Lancaster's nine-year-old niece, a little girl named Catherine, cast the deciding vote.

Captain Raphael Semmes did not pay the yachts much attention as he sailed towards the mouth of the harbor, but the decision of that little girl would save the lives of forty-one of his crew, plus himself.

It took forty-five minutes for the *Alabama* to cover the seven miles out to where the *Kearsarge* lay waiting. During that time Semmes assembled his men and spoke to them all for the first time since that day off the Azores when the *Alabama* was commissioned.

"Officers and Seamen of the *Alabama*! You have, at length, another opportunity of meeting the enemy – the first time that has been presented to you since you sank the Hatteras! In the meantime, you have been all over the world, and it is not too much to say that you have destroyed, and driven for protection under neutral flags, one half of the enemy's commerce, which, at the beginning of the war, covered every sea. This is an achievement for which you may well be proud; and a grateful country will not be unmindful of it. The name of your ship has become a household word wherever civilization extends. Shall that name be tarnished by defeat? The thing is impossible! Remember that you are in the English Channel, the theatre of so much of the naval glory of our race, and that the eyes of Europe are at this moment upon you. The flag that floats over you is that of a young Republic, who bids defiance to her enemies, whenever and wherever found. Show the world that you know how to uphold it! Go to your quarters."

Onboard the **Kearsarge**, Winslow and his crew watched the *Alabama* approach. Winslow's biographer John M. Ellicott wrote:

"After more than a year of tempestuous cruising and blockade, of super-irritating diplomatic wrangle, of physical wear and tear, and of bitter disappointment, a reward for indomitable perseverance was at last in sight, greater than he had ever anticipated. The greatest of Confederate commerce destroyers had been brought to bay and forced to an open fight. She had been sought in vain by twenty-five United States warships, and her pursuit had cost over seven million of dollars. Besides this, there was personality in the coming encounter. Her captain had been Winslow's shipmate, messmate and roommate during a previous war, and his daring, skill and bravery then had well-nigh made him a hero in the eyes of the more modest man. Can it be doubted that, when Winslow focused his glass upon the oncoming *Alabama*, he realized that the supreme moment of his life was at hand? Returning his glass to the quartermaster, he quietly directed his executive to beat to arms."

Winslow had been conducting Sunday services for the crew when one of his quartermasters cried out: "She's coming!"

The battle was about to commence.

When the *Alabama* approached within one nautical mile, the *Kearsarge* turned showing her starboard guns.

The *Alabama* fired first, firing three times. All the shots went wild. The *Kearsarge* turned towards the *Alabama* and approached rapidly, turning again at 900 yards to fire a full broadside. All the shots fell short and the Confederate sailors let loose a loud cheer.

The *Alabama* returned a full broadside sending the shot harmlessly through the rigging of the *Kearsarge*. Winslow attempted to cross the bow of the *Alabama* to send another broadside through the length of the *Alabama*. Semmes was startled at the speed of the Union vessel and barely made his way from under the enemy's guns.

Both ships made seven clockwise circles changing the range from 800 to 1300 yards as a three-knot current drove them both westward. Semmes could not get out of range of Winslow's larger guns nor could he get close enough to board.

Winslow knew that Semmes would have the advantage in a boarding and kept a safe distance from the *Alabama* yet still keeping his enemy in range of his guns.

The Confederates were firing their guns twice as fast as the *Kearsarge* but neither ship scored a hit until twenty minutes into the battle, when the *Alabama* sent a shell into the hull of the *Kearsarge*. It went straight through and lodged in the ship's sternpost.

That one shot would have carried the day for the *Alabama* if only it had exploded. It did not. Semmes later wrote, "If the cap had performed its duty and exploded the shell, I should have been called upon to save Captain Winslow's crew from drowning, instead of his being called upon to save mine. On so slight an incident – the defect of a percussion cap – did the battle hinge. The enemy were very proud of this shell. It was the only trophy they ever got of the *Alabama*."

The *Alabama's* gunners continued to fire. They sent a Blakely shell through the bulwarks of the *Kearsarge* that exploded on the quarterdeck that wounded three of the crew attending the eleven-inch after gun. Two more shots passed through open gun ports without causing any damage. Another shell struck the hammock nettings causing a fire. The forward eleven-inch gun and carriage was toppled but that shell also failed to explode.

Through his glass Semmes could see that his shells were causing insignificant damage, especially the shells striking the hull. He yelled out, "Mr. Kell, our shells strike the enemy's side, doing little damage, and fall off into the water; try solid shot."

Kell alternated between heavy shell and shot but he knew that the obstacle was the heavy chain armor protecting the *Kearsarge*.

The tide was turning. Heavy shells from the Union ship slammed into the *Alabama's* hull. The guns of the *Kearsarge* were ripping the sides of the *Alabama* to pieces. Her rudder was torn apart leaving her without steering and more at mercy to the relentless pounding of the eleven-inch smoothbore cannons of the *Kearsarge.*

An eleven-inch shell tore through a gun-port and exploded killing or wounding nineteen men. Another shot took away the gaff with the ship's colors. With that, the crew of the *Kearsarge* cheered. The Confederates quickly hoisted a new ensign atop the mizzen masthead. More shells hit the deck, killing and wounding more of the *Alabama's* crew. Another shell struck a gun carriage but before it could explode one of the crew grabbed it and tossed it over the side. And then a shell tore through the side of the hull at the waterline and exploded in the engine room.

Despite the carnage the *Alabama's* crew kept fighting. They gave a cheer as one of their hundred-pound shells tore into the engine room of the *Kearsarge*. But this shell also failed to explode and with that, Semmes knew that he would not win the day.

With fire raging through the engine room and water pouring through the breach in the hull, the gallant ship *Alabama* began to list. The *Kearsarge* kept firing, sending shell after shell into the foundering Confederate raider. A fragment of a shell wounded Semmes in the arm. He had it quickly tied off to stop the bleeding but he could see that one by one his guns were falling silent. He had no choice, he had to retreat.

"Mr. Kell, as soon as our head points to the French coast. . . shift your guns to port and make all sail for the coast." Semmes knew that the *Kearsarge* could not carry the attack into French waters.

Winslow anticipated this move and blocked the path of the *Alabama*. His gunners were in a position to rake the decks of the Confederate ship. They did not. Winslow, perhaps out of friendship, belayed the order.

The *Kearsarge* succeeded in blocking the *Alabama's* escape.

Seaman John Roberts went aloft to loose the jib on the *Alabama*. As he was climbing back down, a shell fragment ripped into his abdomen. Roberts clung to the jib boom with his intestines pouring from his gut. In that state he made his way across the footrope to the topgallant deck and climbed to the spar deck. At that point he stopped, stared in amazement at his ghastly wound and screamed as his entrails slid out in a gory mess to rain onto the decks below.

Down below, Dr. Llewellyn was operating on a crew member when a shell ripped through the operating room tearing his patient away from under his blood-stained hands in an explosion of splinters and gore.

The engine room was torn apart and water was pouring into the ship from numerous openings. There was no doubt as Kell reported to Semmes that the *Alabama* was lost. Kell told Semmes, the ship would remain afloat for only another ten minutes at the most.

Semmes in pain and bleeding, answered Kell, "Then sir, cease firing, shorten sail, and haul down the colors. It will never do in the nineteenth century for us to go down and the decks covered with our gallant wounded."

Kell hauled down the colors but the *Kearsarge* fired five more shots after the *Alabama* struck. This caused Kell to order his men back to their guns, but there was nothing they could do. Instead he raised a white flag at the stern and the *Kearsarge* ceased firing.

With captain Semmes dazed and wounded, Kell organized the loading of the wounded into the least damaged quarterboat and sent them under the command of George Fullham to the *Kearsarge*. Kell was angry that no rescue boats were being sent from the **Kearsarge.** He did not know that Winslow did not have any undamaged boats to send.

With the wounded away, Semmes told Kell to give the order to abandon ship and for each man to save himself.

Semmes and Kell were the last to leave along with Semmes's loyal aide Bartelli, sailmaker Alcott and engineer Michael Mars. Mars asked Captain Semmes if there was anything that he could do before leaving the ship. There was. Mars and Bartelli made their way to the captain's partially flooded quarters and secured Semmes's journal and the ship's papers. They wrapped them in oilcloth and brought them on deck taking on the responsibility of protecting them until they could be rescued.

Kell and Semmes both tossed their swords into the channel to prevent them being displayed as Union trophies. All five men then dove into the sea, kicking as strongly as they could to put distance between themselves and the sinking wreck of the **Alabama.**

Semmes was weak, and if not for John Kell he would surely have drowned. Later he would write of his thoughts at that moment. "On the wild waste of waters there came no boats, at first, from the **Kearsarge** to our rescue. Had victory struck them dumb, or helpless – or had it frozen the milk of human kindness in their veins?"

The battle had lasted for an hour and a half. Lieutenant Arthur Sinclair watched as the **Alabama** sank in forty fathoms of water. "The **Alabama's** final plunge was a remarkable freak-, and witnessed by O'Brien and self about one hundred yards off. She shot up out of the water bow first, and descended on the same line, carrying away with her plunge two of her masts, and making a whirlpool of considerable size and strength."

At a safe distance to the west the British yacht **Deerhound** watched the **Alabama** disappear beneath the waves. Young Catherine Lancaster indeed witnessed her sea battle. Just after noon, John Lancaster, seeing the men in the water with no attempts to rescue them, steamed up to the **Kearsarge** to ask why there was no rescue operation underway.

Winslow informed him that he did not have any boats fit to launch. He shouted down from the rails, "For God's sake, do what you can to save them."

Within ten minutes, the *Deerhound's* small boats were making their way through the flotsam to rescue survivors. The chief steward on the Deerhound was William Roberts and he immediately recognized Raphael Semmes. He had met him a few years before in Gibraltar. The semi-conscious Semmes was laid into the stern sheets. He was still bleeding from the gash to his arm.

One of the hastily repaired boats from the *Kearsarge* approached the *Deerhound* and an officer hailed the British crew to ask if there was any sign of Captain Semmes.

A quick-thinking Kell stood up and shouted down, "Captain Semmes is drowned." The Union boat moved on to pick up more survivors.

Lieutenant John McIntosh Kell was with Semmes when the first Confederate raider, the *CCS Sumter,* was launched in 1861 and he had stood with Semmes through the long arduous voyages for over three years that had led them both to this showdown off the coast of France. On this day he not only saved his captain's life from drowning but also saved his freedom from capture.

The *Kearsage* took 70 prisoners including the wounded men delivered by George Fullam. Winslow ordered Fullham to return and gather more survivors but this time Fullham delivered them and himself to the *Deerhound*. The *Deerhound* took on 42 men including 12 officers.

Arthur Sinclair and another man were rescued by a boat from the *Kearsarge* but managed to slip back over the side to swim to one of the *Deerhound's* boats. Fifteen more men were taken onboard two French pilot boats. One boat delivered the men as prisoners to the Union cruiser and the other landed the *Alabama* men to freedom in France.

Nine men from the *Alabama* had been killed in action and another twelve had drowned. A total of 21 dead and 21 wounded including Captain Semmes.

The *Kearsarge* suffered only one death and three wounded.

John Lancaster approached Raphael Semmes where he had been taken below and wrapped in blankets.

"I think every man is saved, where shall I land you?"

Semmes smiled, and without hesitation replied, "I am under English colors, the sooner you land me on English soil, the better."

Lancaster accepted this and requested the skipper of the *Deerhound*, Captain Evan Jones, to set a course for Southhampton.

Gideon Welles was incensed that Semmes had escaped but there was not much he could do to chastise Winslow who had become a national hero. He sent Winslow a letter of congratulations and the announcement that President Lincoln had promoted Winslow to the rank of Commodore.

John Lancaster received a letter of gratitude from Confederate President Jefferson Davis and a Joint Letter of Appreciation from the Congress of the Confederacy. Despite protests from Charles Francis Adams that Lancaster be censured by the British Government, Lord Russell stated that Lancaster deserved praise for his actions. Lord Russell stated quite firmly to the United States that the British government was never under any obligation to return escaped prisoners to the United States that were on British soil.

Raphael Semmes recovered within a week of landing in Britain. He paid off his men and set aside funds to cover the survivors who were not landed with him from the *Deerhound*. A group of admiring officers in the Royal Navy presented him with a sword to replace the one he had thrown into the English Channel. Semmes then spent six weeks touring Europe before making his way home to the South.

Gideon Welles was determined and even desperate to capture Semmes. He put the navy on notice that Semmes was coming home and he intended to catch him running the blockade. In this Semmes eluded the Union once again. Instead of attempting to run the blockade, he made his way to Mexico landing at Matamoros. He then took a small boat across the Rio Grande to Brownsville, Texas, and then made his way home to Richmond.

Mallory promoted Semmes to rear admiral on February 10, 1865, and he was given command of the James River Squadron. With the fall of Richmond, Semmes destroyed his ironclads and took his naval brigade to Danville, Virginia, to join President Jefferson Davis and Mallory. There he was given the commission as a brigadier general, becoming the only man in the Civil War on either side to hold both the rank of rear admiral of the navy and brigadier general of the army.

On May 1, 1865, Semmes surrendered to Union General William Hartsuff in Greensboro, North Carolina.

He was now a civilian but Gideon Welles was not done with him. Welles wanted his revenge and on December 15, 1865, soldiers arrested him at his home in Mobile, Alabama. He was charged with violating the "usages of war" by escaping after surrendering to the *Kearsarge* and then later resuming his military actions against the Union.

Semmes was held for four months in prison as Welles pleaded with President Andrew Johnson to sign an executive order to place Semmes on trial. Johnson refused and Semmes was released. Welles then tried to press charges of piracy, privateering, treason and the inhumane treatment of prisoners against Semmes.

For Welles it was a personal vendetta. No other Confederate officer had caused Welles so much trouble, expense and embarrassment as Semmes had.

Finally, President Andrew Johnson officially proclaimed the war at an end on April 3, 1866, and Raphael Semmes was given a full pardon and freedom from trial.

The most effective commerce raider of the war had survived. He had cost the Union nearly five million dollars in damages to maritime commerce and had destroyed some fifty-four ships including numerous whalers and their cargoes of whale oil.

In total the *Alabama* had sunk 16 whalers setting a new record for whaling ships destroyed. The previous record had been held by the New England commodore David Porter, who in command of the frigate *Essex* had destroyed numerous British whalers in the Pacific during the War of 1812.

Raphael Semmes died in Mobile, Alabama, on August 30, 1877, at the age of 68. Commerce raider, accused pirate, U.S. and Confederate naval captain, Confederate rear admiral and brigadier general, lawyer and writer. His career was best summed up with words with which he addressed President Jefferson Davis: "Whatever else may be said of me, I have, at least, brought no discredit upon the American name and character."

I can sympathize with Raphael Semmes and the government's efforts to penalize him for his actions during the war. For my own actions against illegal Japanese whaling I have been persecuted by the government of Japan and accused of being a pirate by a 9th District Court judge in the United States, an accusation that was brought against me by a 9th Circuit Court Federal Judge without due process. There was never a trial nor evidence presented, just an opinion of a judge favoring the request of the Japanese whalers for an injunction to stop our interventions against illegal Japanese whaling in the Southern Ocean.

CHAPTER X

The Launch of the *Shenandoah*

It was the intention of the Confederacy to deliberately destroy the Yankee whaling fleet.

On September 28, 1864, James D. Bulloch's request for Lieutenant R.R. Carter to come to Britain from Richmond was answered.

It was Carter who had approached the Secretary of the Confederate Navy with the idea of getting a ship to directly attack the Yankee whaling fleets. He brought to Bulloch a set of "Whale Charts" published within the report of the project labelled "Physical Geography of the Sea."

While serving with the United States Navy, Carter had participated in a scientific expedition that had amongst other things mapped out the areas and the courses taken by American whaling ships.

The charts had been compiled by Commander Matthew Fontaine Maury who had resigned from the U.S. Navy to join with the Confederate Navy. Maury presented the charts to Carter to deliver to Bulloch in Great Britain.

Maury's charts were the first published charts on whale migrations and had been very valuable to the Yankee whalers. The charts were also available to the Confederate raiders. The charts that were being used to find and hunt the whales would in turn be used to hunt and find the whalers.

Bulloch requested of Carter that he prepare a memorandum containing the information as a guidance for the commander of the ship he was preparing for the mission to hunt whalers.

Lieutenant William C. Whittle was a Confederate officer with whom I could readily identify. He and I were about the same age when we began our wars against the whalers, he as the first officer on the Confederate raider *Shenandoah* in 1864 and I as first officer on the *Greenpeace V* in 1975.

Despite his youth, Whittle was selected by James Bulloch to be the chief executive officer under Captain James I. Waddell.

Bulloch could not have chosen a more deserving man. At twenty years of age, Whittle had been a junior officer on the *Nashville*, the first Confederate ship to run the blockade to England and back again to Beaufort, North Carolina. With the Union army advancing in Beaufort and with Union cruisers offshore, Whittle was ordered to burn the *Nashville*.

He did not. Instead he defied his orders and left port with only a quarter of a crew. In the dark of night, he sped dangerously across the bar at fourteen knots. When the Union cruisers spotted him, he steered his ship straight between the two cruisers knowing they could not open fire without the risk of hitting each other. He then outran the Union ships and delivered the *Nashville* safely into Georgetown as a hero.

Three years later, as a Confederate spy in Liverpool, Lieutenant William C. Whittle was given the task of boarding an English ship called the *Sea King,* just before she slipped down the Mersey River.

He boarded as a coal agent under the name of George Brown.

That evening another ship was preparing to sail. A messenger ran through the foggy night calling in at hotels and boarding houses to deliver tickets for a British steamship bound for Nassau in the Bahamas called the *Laurel.*

Most of the men were teenagers or in their early twenties. There were a few veterans who had survived the sinking of the *Alabama*. None of them knew their destination except for one man, the eldest man in the group, James Iredell Waddell.

Waddell was a seasoned American naval officer. He had seen action at Vera Cruz during the Mexican War. When hostilities broke out between the North and the South, he resigned his commission.

In a letter to the Secretary of the Navy he wrote, "I wish to be understood that no doctrine of the right of secession, no wish for disunion of the States impels me, but simply because my home is the home of my people in the South, and I cannot bear arms against it or them."

As the *Laurel* moved down the Crosby Channel with the tide, James D. Bulloch stood on a Liverpool hill and watched her until she was out of sight.

Only three men knew the mission of both the *Sea King* and the *Laurel.* Whittle on the *Sea King*, Waddell on the *Laurel* and Bulloch.

Bulloch had pulled it off. He had secured a new raider and officers and crew to man her.

On the *Laurel*, Waddell opened a letter from Bulloch:

> "You are about to proceed upon a cruise in the far-distant Pacific, into the sea and among the islands frequented by the Great American whaling fleet, a source of abundant wealth to our enemies and a nursery for their seamen. It is hoped that you may be able to greatly damage and disperse that fleet, even if you do not succeed in utterly destroying it."

The *Shenandoah* was thus the first of the raiders to be specifically instructed to search out and destroy whaling vessels.

Bulloch had organized and deployed his plan with meticulous care and secrecy but as he stood upon that hill he was troubled with anxiety. He knew the USS *Niagara* was patrolling in the English Channel. He was not troubled by the *Sea King*. Except for Whittle, the crew were British and knew nothing of the particulars of the plan and there was nothing suspicious that could be found onboard her.

The *Laurel* on the other hand carried a cargo of armaments and enough crew to outfit a cruiser.

The USS *Niagara* actually passed the *Sea King* while chasing a Spanish vessel they suspected of carrying arms and within a matter of days the Union spies had discovered that a large cargo of arms had been loaded onto the *Laurel* along with suspected Confederate sailors. The *Laurel* was also rumored to have taken on Captain Raphael

Semmes. The Union Navy was now on the hunt for a suspected new Confederate raider.

Once clear of the channel, the *Laurel* set course for Madeira arriving ahead of the *Sea King*.

Just before arrival at Funchal, Captain Corbett advised the men that George Brown, the coal agent, would now be in charge.

Both ships rendezvoused to an uninhabited island south of Madeira called Las Desertas.

George Brown stepped onboard the *Laurel* to greet Captain Waddell.

"I am very happy to see you, Lieutenant Whittle. How is the ship?"

"A good sailor," said Whittle with a smile.

All hands from both ships plus some impressed Portuguese fishermen began to shift the cargo from the *Laurel* to the *Sea King* and were very much surprised to see that the boxes marked machinery were cannons and arms.

When all the guns and supplies were onboard, the crew were ordered to the aft deck of the *Sea King* where Captain Corbett was standing in his black merchant uniform and beside him James I. Waddell in the grey and gold uniform of the Confederacy.

Corbett was blunt. "Well men, I have sold this ship to the Confederates. She is to belong to their Navy to be a cruiser and burn and destroy merchant ships and whalers. She is not to fight, men, but only to capture prizes. There will be a first-rate chance for any of you young men who will stop by the vessel. All of you men who like to join, I'll give you two months' wages. And this gentleman" turning towards Waddell, "is offering good wages. Four pounds a month for able seamen, and ten pounds bounty for joining up. As you are all young men, I advise you to join her, as you will make a fine thing of it. Step forward those who will."

There were no volunteers.

British quartermaster John Ellison shouted out, "I agreed with you in London to go to Bombay, Cap'n...you sir, have broken your agreement. Why are we not proceeding to Bombay?"

"Well men, I cannot help it."

"What of us who do not join?" asked one of the confused seamen.

"You can come back with me to England," Corbett answered.

Unfortunately for Waddell almost all of the English sailors elected to return to England on the **Laurel**. He had but only 19 + 23 = 42 to man a vessel requiring 150 hands.

Lieutenant Whittle assured Waddell that the men would be able to run the ship until they could recruit more hands. They were young and dedicated and confident and to a man informed Captain Waddell that they were ready to take to the ocean.

Captain Waddell read the articles commissioning the ship as the Cruiser **Shenandoah**, Confederate States Navy. The date of commissioning was October 19, 1864.

Undermanned and lacking adequate supplies, including missing gun tackles, the **Shenandoah** headed south capturing Yankee ships with which to supply needed stores. The gun tackles were supplied by the **Alena** on October 30th before she was scuttled.

On November 6th, the schooner **Charter Oak** was burned. On November 8th, the bark **D. Godfrey** was burned. On November 10th, the brig **Susan** was scuttled. On November 12th, the ships **Kate Prince** and **Adelaide** were bonded. On November 13th, the schooner **Lizzie M. Stacey** was burned.

Seven prizes in two weeks, two scuttled, two bonded and three burned.

Two more weeks went by without any captures until December 4th when the whaler **Edward** was taken.

I also had the experience of secretly purchasing and delivering a ship from a foreign nation, the difference being that in our case it was an enemy nation – Japan.

In 2012, I secured a new ship (Seifu Maru) for our fleet right under the noses of the Japanese whalers. Being made aware that the Japanese government was selling one of their research ships, I conspired with Lockhart MacLean and Peter Rysman to purchase her.

Of course, Japan was not about to sell Sea Shepherd one of their ships, so we registered a company in Delaware in the United States

that in turn established a second company in Hong Kong. We then found a Korean broker to arrange the inspection and the sail. We named the ship the "New Atlantis" and also arranged for the Japanese crew to deliver the vessel into our hands in Cairns, Australia.

Our new ship was then named the *Sam Simon* after the co-creator of the Simpsons.

The *Sam Simon* was made ready and participated in Operation Zero Tolerance where, along with our ships *Brigitte Bardot, Steve Irwin* and *Bob Barker,* and cut the Japanese whale kill quota by 90%.

CHAPTER XI

Edward

December 4, 1864

The bark rigged 400-ton *Edward* was an old whaling ship and the blood of a thousand whales had seeped into her every nook, crack and seam. Built in 1818 originally as a merchant ship she was soon after enlisted into the whaling industry and for almost a half a century she had been a floating abattoir, stinking of rancid oil and decaying flesh.

She was one of the ships that had nearly wiped out the once abundant populations of Sperm whales, first working out of Nantucket and then moving on to the New England whale oil capital of New Bedford. She had hunted down and slaughtered whales in the South Pacific, and in the even more remote waters of the Arctic and Antarctic.

The *Edward* was a ship of death.

The *Edward* had escaped the purchase of forty other old whalers by the federal government as part of the conscription for the Great Stone Fleet that the U.S. Navy had scuttled outside of Southern harbors as part of the strategic blockade of Confederate ports.

In the early afternoon of December 3, 1864, the crew of the *Edward* were pulling on the oars of their whaleboats as they closed in on a defenseless Right whale. The whale sounded but the experienced whalers knew how long she would be under, what course she would take and where to be ready for her when she surfaced.

When she did, the whaleboat was upon her. The harpooner stood up in the bow holding the deadly iron in his right hand. He hurled it into her backside and joyfully watched as the great animal reacted with immediate shock as the razor-sharp blade painfully violated her flesh. In agony she slammed the sea with her broad tail and surged forward, blood streaming from the ugly wound in her back. The white hemp rope shot out of the barrel and over the rollers as the harpooner traded places with an officer armed with a four-pound blunderbuss loaded with a foot-long shell with a short fuse.

The dying whale pulled the men in their relatively small boat for two miles before she once again sounded and disappeared into the depths. Her tormentors waited on the surface for her to rise and when she did, the officer pulled the trigger and sent the deadly explosive shell deep into her body and within seconds heard the muffled explosion as her internal organs were torn and shredded.

At the same time, the great mammal's head rose from the water with a scream, as twin plumes of dark red blood snorted skyward from her spout, showering the men with her hot blood as she took her final mortal breath, choking on her own lifeblood as the whaling men cheered in excited triumph without a trace of sympathy or compassion.

It was the first whale killed since leaving New Bedford four months before and it would be their last cry of joy for inflicting death on their voyage as it would be the last whale the *Edward* would ever again slay.

Vengeance was on the horizon in the shape of a sleek black cruiser.

Since the taking of the *Alina* on October 30, 1864, Captain Waddell had scuttled two ships (*Alina* and *Susan*), bonded two others (*Kate Prince* and *Adelaide*) and burnt three more (*Charter Oak, D. Godfrey* and *Lizzie M. Stacey*).

These merchant ship prizes although of no impact to the whaling industry certainly increased the readiness and the comfort of the *Shenandoah* for her mission. The crew quarters were now well outfitted with tables and chairs. The wardroom library now held over

600 volumes and the eight staterooms were now very comfortable quarters for the officers.

When first taking command of the *Shenandoah*, Captain Waddell had described the master's cabin as "the most cheerless and offensive spot I ever occupied." Thanks to the luxuries taken from the merchant ships it was now carpeted with expensive furnishings, a very good library and an impressive collection of fine wine.

The *Shenandoah's* objective was the whaling grounds of the Pacific and as she headed ever southward in the South Atlantic, the crew sighted Inaccessible Island of the Tristan da Cunha group. These volcanic islands sit midway between South America and Africa, 1,400 miles south from St Helena, the closest landfall, and 1,700 miles west of Cape Town, South Africa.

Waddell and his officers were very much aware that Tristan da Cunha was a popular place for whalers to stop.

Late in the afternoon of December 4th, a bark was spotted and there was no doubt she was a Yankee whaler.

The whalers were so occupied with cutting up their latest victim that they failed to see the approaching raider until she was upon them and even then, they did not see a threat.

The bark *Edward* hailed the *Shenandoah* and not imaging it to be a Confederate raider, proudly ran up the star-spangled banner.

A collective shock and a shudder ran through the entire crew when the large black ship raised the dreaded Stars and Bars.

A very disappointed Captain Charles Worth resigned to his misfortune, stood by the rails as the Confederate boarding party arrived. His crew had stopped their bloody work of cutting out a large Right whale tied alongside. Blood ran into the scuppers and huge chunks of blubber called "bible leaves" were piled upon the deck. Black smoke was rising from the try pots as the fires beneath them were fed with the same blubber being tossed into the rendering pots.

The boarding party invited Captain Worth to return to the *Shenandoah* with his papers and he did so with a stoic acceptance of his fate. There was no disputing her ownership. She was a Yankee whaler and fair game for the Confederate raider.

And as she had just embarked on a three-year voyage she was well stocked with supplies. She was also the answer to all of Waddell's needs containing large stores of provisions sealed in whale oil barrels and most importantly, all the rope, pulley and blocks needed to rig the guns on the *Shenandoah*.

Captain Worth gained the respect of the rebels with his calm acceptance of the capture. When he had first come aboard the *Shenandoah*, he greeted Captain Waddell, Lt. Whittle and John Berkley Grimball politely saying, "Good afternoon gentlemen, you have a fine ship here for a cruiser."

Grimball replied, "Yes sir, and that vessel of yours looks as if she is familiar with traveling salt water."

Worth looked over at his lost ship, the large carcass of the mutilated whale still lashed to her side. "Yes, she was laid on the stocks before you or I were thought of."

The *Shenandoah* spent two days alongside the *Edward* off-loading their prize. The provisions included 200 barrels of beef and pork, 46 barrels of flour, 2 tons of ship's biscuits, 600 pounds of coffee and 400 pounds of butter. They also took 1,200 pounds of soap, a large quantity of tobacco and a very large stock of clothing and canvas in addition to the ropes and tackle.

They also captured three very sturdy whale boats to replace the inferior boats onboard the *Shenandoah*.

It was also the first time that the Confederate crew aside from Joshua Minor, had seen the workings of a whaler up close and they were not impressed.

"A dead whale is no nosegay, it is an offensive exhalation too horrible to relate," wrote Waddell in his logbook.

Dr. Charles Lining went onboard to see first-hand the mutilated whale. "Blubber," he reported, "was much as I imagined it, but not so thick. It had a horrid smell and as the ship was greasy, I soon satisfied myself and came off."

The death of the *Edward* was a spectacular sight. An old wooden ship saturated with five decades of whale oil, tar, kerosene paint and turpentine was ripe for nursing the flames that Bulloch, Minor and George Harwood applied to her fore and aft. After setting her afire, they retreated back to the deck of the *Shenandoah* to watch her burn.

The flames crawled across the deck and snaked up the rigging into the sheets, becoming increasingly brighter as the ship burned an intense fiery orange under an inky billowing of thick ebony smoke.

As Whittle described it, "Our burning prize is distinctly in sight, and I have rarely seen anything which is more beautifully grand than a ship burning at sea. To see the rigging on fire, after it gets burnt in two and the burning ends swinging as the vessel rolls – oh it is a grand sight."

The burning hulk was also a funeral pyre for the remains of the slain Right whale and her oily blubber. That, along with the oil in the try pots on deck and in the hogsheads below deck, sent ghastly, greasy smoke to the sky while at the same time destroying the harpoons and lances that would never again be used.

Although the whaler was valued at only $20,000, her stores were most welcome by the Confederates and her demise insured that many whales would live because of her fiery destruction.

Satisfied that the flames had utterly condemned the *Edward*, the *Shenandoah* steamed off into the darkness as the burning hulk directly astern, slowly disappeared below the horizon.

The crew of the whaler consisted of Captain Worth, three mates and twenty-two seamen. Only one of the whalers consented to join the *Shenandoah* and Waddell accepted him as he was a skilled carpenter and cooper but would have been inclined to reject the rest of them if they had wanted to join. Captain Worth was paroled and allowed the freedom to go about the ship, the rest were confined in irons. Waddell sensed that they would be trouble. Most were Portuguese and could not speak English and all were unhappy about losing their livelihoods.

With his small crew, Waddell was justifiably concerned that his prisoners could overpower his men and take the ship. He had no other choice then to deposit them on nearby Tristan da Cunha despite the possibility of a Yankee warship arriving in their search for them.

Because of this concern Waddell did not drop anchor but steamed through the thick kelp beds and into Falmouth Bay where the prisoners were put into the longboats to be ferried to the beach.

After six weeks at sea, the smell of land was intoxicating for the crew and they hungered to go ashore. Tristan da Cunha is a magnificent sight. From the dormant volcanic cone, the verdant land rippled in small hills down the slopes. The crew looked up in awe at the five-hundred-foot-high basalt walls that dropped down to the sea. On the Northern side, however, a valley cut its way down to the shoreline and it was there that a small group of stone houses with grassy roofs nestled safely back from the shore partially obscured by the morning fog that was slowing burning away. In front of one of the houses the Union Jack hung limply from a pole although the ownership of the islands was still in question.

Only thirty-five inhabitants resided on the one island of Tristan da Cunha itself. The other two islands, Nightingale and Inaccessible, were uninhabited. This small population was remarkably quite diverse with men and women who had originated from New England, South Africa, Britain, Portugal, and the Netherlands.

It was a Dutchman named Peter Groen who had Anglicized his name to Peter Green after being shipwrecked there in 1836 who was the appointed de facto governor of the tiny colony.

Green was a red-faced stocky man with a beard down to his waist.

Green and the other inhabitants of the little colony were mystified at the approach of the *Shenandoah*. They did not recognize the flag and they had never before seen whalers landed on their shores as prisoners.

Cornelius Hunt wrote, "It was the first time that any of the Islanders had seen the flag that floated at our peak, and to what nationality it belonged they could not imagine. Nor was their astonishment in any way diminished when we informed them that our ship was a Confederate cruiser, and we had thirty-five prisoners which we proposed contributing to their population."

"And where did you get these prisoners?" asked Green.

"From a whaler not far from here," replied one of the officers from the *Shenandoah*.

"Just so, to be sure, and what became of the whaler?"

"We burned her."

"Whew! Is that the way you dispose of what vessels you fall in with?"

"If they belong to the United States; not otherwise."

"Well, my hearty, you know your business, but my notion is that these sort of pranks will get you into the devil's own muss before you're through with it. What your quarrel with the United States is I don't know, but I swear I don't believe they will stand for this kind of work."

At first Green protested that Waddell had no right to land his prisoners on British territory as he pointed to the Jack on the pole in front of his house. Waddell requested that Green produce papers to prove that the islands were under British authority. Green could not produce any such papers.

Captain Waddell then negotiated with Green to take his prisoners and provided for them a ton of flour, four barrels of pork and four barrels of beef. Surgeon Lining wrote, "because I did not want it ever said that we left them on a nearly destitute isle to the charity of such poor people."

The *Shenandoah* purchased fresh food and meat from the islanders at high prices and sold them flour at low prices and with the barter complete, the raider made ready to depart leaving the whalers ashore.

For the whales, the American Civil War was good news. The cruises of the Confederate raiders had spread fear across the briny waters of the world. This was confirmed for Waddell when he inquired of islander Peter Green if he had seen any other whalers in the area. Green replied that very few whalers had called in at the island for some time.

"Ye have yourselves to thank for that. Before the war it was common to count as many as seventy whalers in sight of the islands at times. Now it is rare to sight a single one."

Whittle smiled and said, "It is wonderful that even here in this remote island, away entirely from our country, that people feel the effect of the war in our country. This proves to us our importance."

Waddell wasted little time negotiating the business of off-loading the prisoners and loading fresh provisions. By 14:00 hours, with a light breeze coming out of the northwest, he gave orders to get underway. He set a course of "east by north and a half north" so that the islanders and the prisoners would think he was bound for Cape Town. As soon as he was well over the horizon he changed the course to "south by east and a quarter east" and headed into the "Roaring Forties." The *Shenandoah* was bound for the South Pacific with a route underneath Australia, well away from any searching United States warships.

On December 28, 1864, the United States warship *Iroquois* stopped briefly at Tristan da Cunha to inquire about the *Shenandoah*. Hearing the news that the Confederates were seen on a course bound for Cape Town, Captain Rodgers quickly took on the prisoners and the *Iroquois* set off on a fruitless voyage to Southern Africa. Three weeks behind, with limited coal and a top speed of 7 knots, the U.S. steamer was at a serious disadvantage in this chase even if Captain Waddell had not avoided Cape Town altogether.

Chapter XII

A Warm Reception in Williamstown

Williamstown, Victoria, Australia
January 25, 1864

From 2005 through 2013, my ships and crew have utilized Australia as our base of operations to intervene against the Japanese whaling fleet operating in the Southern Ocean. At first, we were given a free berth at Victoria docklands in Melbourne, and then later, a permanent base of operations at the Seaworks docks in Williamstown.

In December 2007, when we first berthed in Williamstown, I was walking along the street and was amazed to discover a wall mural depicting the Confederate raider *Shenandoah*.

As I looked out across Port Phillip Bay, I could see in my mind's eye the great black Confederate raider being guided by a pilot to this very place where my own ship, the black-hulled *Steve Irwin*, was now berthed. The Confederate ship had been in the same harbor one hundred and forty years ago and much had changed, but the mural was testament to the fact that the visit of the *Shenandoah* had not been forgotten.

Edward Johnson, the Port Phillips pilot, boarded the *Shenandoah* at noon on January 25, 1865. "Why do you want to get into the harbor?" he asked Waddell.

Annoyed by the question, Waddell responded, "Why do you ask, Sir?"

"No offense, Captain, but my orders is rigid about belligerent cruisers. They has got to have a reason to come into harbor."

Waddell explained that he was in need of repairs and thus satisfied, the pilot agreed to take the cruiser on to Melbourne.

Cornelius E. Hunt had recorded that entrance, and wrote: "On the 25th, ninety days out from Madeira, we sighted land, and a few hours later we passed through Port Philip Heads, the entrance to Hobson's Bay. Here the pilot boarded us, and was very much astonished was that functionary, when he learned the name and character of the vessel he had in charge, which it seemed had been reported as the ship **Royal Standard**, fifty odd days out from London. This erroneous impression was soon corrected by a telegraph, and we steamed on up the Bay at the rate of nine knots an hour, passing a multitude of yachts, and pleasure boats of various descriptions, filled with an eager multitude, all apparently delighted to see such a ship with the Confederate flag flying, and about six o'clock, we dropped anchor off Sandridge, a small town about two miles from Melbourne."

In a similar fashion were my ships *Farley Mowat*, *Bob Barker*, *Gojira/Brigitte Bardot*, *Sam Simon* and *Robert Hunter/Steve Irwin* greeted by yachts and cheering Australians over the past few years, although for different reasons. But the Confederate raider and my vessels did have one thing very much in common in that we were hunters of whalers.

The support of the Australians for the Confederates was strong and enthusiastic. According to Whittle, the *Shenandoah* was given a hero's welcome, just as my ships were every time given the same when we entered an Australian port nearly a century and a half later.

"We passed on with our flag flying, numerous steamers, tugs and sailing craft saluted by dipping their ensigns and in some instances by cheering. All greetings were heartfelt and were returned cheerfully."

Waddell added in his journal, "Cheer after cheer greeted us from the generous, brave-hearted Englishmen and Australians, who believed in the justice of our cause."

I marveled at the similarities between the way my crews and I were welcomed and the description by Hunt of the reception the *Shenandoah* had received.

"As soon as it became generally known in Melbourne that a Confederate cruiser had arrived in the offing, a scene of excitement was inaugurated which baffles all adequate description. Crowds of people were rushing hither and thither, seeking authentic information concerning the stranger, and ere we had been an hour at anchor, a perfect fleet of boats was pulling toward us from every direction.

"The *Shenandoah* was thrown open to the inspection of visitors.

"As soon as this was known, and the news seemed to spread like wildfire, steamers and sailboats came flocking off towards us, and all day long, and until far into the evening, were plying between our ship and the shore, bringing on board and taking away thousands of persons, all eager to say that they had visited the famous 'rebel pirate.'

"The multitude of absurd questions with which we were plied by the gaping crowd, would have made a stoic laugh. A large percentage of our visitors seemed to entertain the notion that the human beings were removed from the vessels we captured, or not, as convenience dictated, prior to their destruction, and solemnly queried of us to the manner in which the Yankees bore themselves while watching the approach of the devouring element upon a burning ship, or waiting to be engulfed with a scuttled one. But not withstanding this hard character they were ready to ascribe to us, they vied with each other in showing every courtesy in their power, and the ladies in particular were well pleased when they could secure the attendance of a grey uniform to escort them on their tour of inspection. Of a truth there are some curious phases in human nature.

"The following day we were the recipients of some more tangible proof of the goodwill with which the residents of Melbourne regarded us. Each of our officers received a railroad pass to go and return from Sandridge to Melbourne on the Hobson Bay Railroad, so long as we remained in port. Invitations to dinners and balls poured in from all sides, and every one was particular to mention that he felt the warmest sympathy for the Confederate cause.

"All of this was agreeable enough if one did not care to examine too closely the sincerity of these friendly demonstrations, and after ninety days at sea, it was pleasant to see the gay groups of women upon our decks, but the *Shenandoah* had come to refit, not to be exhibited as a curiosity, and this continual crush and whirl of visitors put an effectual check to the real business in hand; consequently, when the first excitement had in a measure subsided, we were obliged to close our doors, and hang out a most inhospitable and peremptory "not at home" to all callers. This prohibition caused considerable heart-burnings, but necessity knows no law, and upon the whole, our popularity did not suffer.

"But after all, that tarry in Melbourne was one of the bright reminiscences of our adventurous cruise round the world. I do not suppose so much hospitality ever was or ever will be shown to another ship in that port, and there were few if any who sailed in the *Shenandoah*, who will not carry to their graves many pleasant memories of the days they spent on the shores of Australia."

It is pleasing that in fact, my ships have indeed been given a much greater reception. But given that the population is much larger, and that our cause of stopping Japanese whaling is very much a cause that the Australians enthusiastically embrace, we can share with the Confederate sailors the fact that the Australians are indeed friendly and hospitable people.

Another striking similarity was that in both the visit of the *Shenandoah* and the visits of the Sea Shepherd ships, the Australian public was very supportive, whereas the Australian authorities were less so.

Public support was so strong that although the Australian government were under considerable pressure then by the American Consul with regard to the Confederates, and today by the Japanese Embassy in regard to whale defenders, they could do nothing more than make a show of appearing to be strict with the visiting vessels.

In our case, this was simply an annual routine raid by the Australian Federal police in a fruitless effort to secure evidence of wrongdoing at the request of Japan. It was all very dramatic but of no consequence. They did interfere with our importing bullet-proof vests which are illegal under Australian law mostly due to the legendary Australian outlaw Ned Kelly, whose gang had worn armor during shoot-outs with the constables.

Being that our ships were not warships, we could not claim immunity to the searches but the crew could refuse to answer the questions put to them by the Australian Federal Police and did exactly that.

In fact, it became an expected routine for us to be searched by the Australian Federal Police at the conclusion of every campaign. They were acting on requests by the Japanese police and went through the motions but there never really was much enthusiasm by the police to do Japan's bidding and nothing much ever came from the searches.

In a similar fashion with regard to the Confederates, the British were seen to be enforcing the neutrality act with regards to the *Shenandoah*, but not interfering with repairs, fueling and provisioning. They were, however, interfering with the recruitment of seamen.

The Australian government then, as now, was caught between a rock and a hard place. Then the people were in sympathy with the Confederates but the government had to maintain a policy of neutrality and at the same time appease the Union and the Union-sympathizers. With myself it was the same story with the people overwhelmingly in support of our anti-whaling efforts against the Japanese whalers in the Southern Ocean and pressure from the Japanese government to detain us and prevent us from returning to sea.

Governor Sir Charles Henry Darling made the decision to allow the Shenandoah to undergo repairs and land prisoners but maintained that recruitment of crew would not be allowed.

With permission received, Australians flocked to the *Shenandoah* and were allowed to come onboard and visit with the crew. The local people were thrilled to set foot onboard the Raider and many Australians opened their homes to the Confederate crew members or took them out to the pubs and bought them drinks.

"Invitation after invitation has already been extended to us and the hospitality of the people is apparently only surpassed by their immeasurable curiosity," Whittle wrote.

My experiences paralleled those of the Confederates even more so with tens of thousands of people visiting and touring our ships in Melbourne, Williamstown, Hobart, Fremantle, Sydney, Brisbane and honorary port status given to us by Fremantle, Williamstown and Melbourne.

At the same time, the Federal Australian government has for years taken a passive-aggressive stance with us, harassing us when they can, denying us tax exempt status, attempting to deny visas and constant harassment by customs and immigration officials.

The fact remains, however, that without the incredible support of the people of Australia, Sea Shepherd would not have achieved the success we have in our interventions against the whalers.

And without the support of the people of Victoria, the *Shenandoah* would not have been able to return to sea to continue their aggressive efforts in destroying the whaling fleets.

Melbourne in 1865 was just three decades old with a population of around 50,000. The colony shared with Great Britain an aversion to slavery but at the same time a good number of people harbored admiration and respect for the rights of the Confederate states to secede.

The political views ranged from enthusiastic support for the Rebels to angry opposition from Yankee expatriates, the latter allied strangely enough with a curious group of British conspiracy theorists that believed Australia was about to be attacked by imperialist armies from North America.

An editorial in the *Sydney Morning Herald* warned: "There is no doubt that the chance of invasion of this country by American privateers has roused the spirit of self-defense."

This nationalist paranoia started to fester in Australia as early as 1856. By 1862 the Parliament in Victoria had already spent close to a million pounds on harbor defenses. Nonetheless it was not an efficient defense. When the Russian warship *Bogatyr* arrived for an official visit and presented a salute with their cannons, the Queenscliff battery was unable to reply because they had neglected to purchase gunpowder for their guns.

But pointing guns at the Confederates was the last thing on Aussie minds. The Southern rebels were welcomed with open arms by most of the population, and this was due in part to all the romantic tales they had heard about the exploits of the *Alabama*. There were even rumors that the most notorious sailor of the day, Captain Raphael Semmes, was onboard the *Shenandoah*.

There were real dangers. Yankees and Yankee sympathizers were angry seeing the Confederate raider sitting brazenly at anchor in the port of Melbourne. A Union merchant ship, the *Mustang* out of New York, was anchored closed by in Hobson's Bay and her captain and some of his crew decided to take action despite their status as merchantmen. They constructed a torpedo filled with one hundred kilos of gunpowder and placed it alongside the hull of the *Shenandoah* in the dead of night. The trigger was a long line that ran through the water back to the *Mustang*. When the line was pulled, it broke and the torpedo failed to explode. The Yankees apparently lost their nerve and did not attempt a second act of sabotage.

My ship *Bob Barker*, berthed in Hobart, also suffered a bomb threat. A call to the Hobart police warned that a bomb had been placed on the Sea Shepherd ship. The police came to the *Bob Barker* with a request to abandon ship. No bomb was found, but the call came from a Melbourne-registered cell phone and the man responsible was located, arrested, and fined.

Captain Waddell and his officers were not much cheered by the newspaper reports they were reading. The three Melbourne newspapers, the *Age,* the *Herald* and the *Argus,* all contained articles from the home front and for the Confederates it was not good news.

The Southern forces had retreated from the Shenandoah Valley and there was little standing in the way of General William Tecumseh Sherman's army from advancing into Georgia. The fall of Savannah was imminent.

The South were resorting to guerilla warfare and the only news that gave them cause to smile were the reports of the successes of Mosby's raiders in Virginia and a report of ten thousand Confederate troops under General Breckenridge routing the Union army from Bull's Gap, Tennessee.

More ominous were the reports that the **Florida** had been sunk leaving the **Shenandoah** as the only Confederate raider remaining active on the high seas.

The three newspapers expressed different points of view regarding the arrival of the **Shenandoah**.

The Age was strongly pro-Union and they wasted little time making their bias known to the public: "We cannot regard the Shenandoah as other than a marauding craft, and her officers and crew then a gang of respectable pirates…. Her vocation is not to fight, but to plunder; not to vanquish enemies in fair struggle, but to destroy unarmed antagonists; not to shed the blood of her crew in their country's defense, but to fill their pockets with prize money."

The *Herald* retaliated, making reference to Captain Waddell's ship being manned by: "A fine and determined looking set of officers." And with regard to the crew: "A happy and apparently well contented lot who express great confidence in their commander and are well pleased with the service in which they are engaged."

The *Herald* did acknowledge that the role of the **Shenandoah** was to "burn, sink, and plunder," but added, "we cannot but recognize and fraternize with the brave men who uphold their country's flag at the risk of being hanged at the yard-arm."

The *Argus* joined the fray with an editorial slamming Lincoln: "A government which has kept no faith with her enemies and wherever it has been possible to do so with safety, has broken every promise to its friends – a government which under the pretext of a Crusade against slavery, has committed crimes against civilization more deplorable than slavery."

The media took sides with the Sea Shepherd's war against the whalers beginning in Australia in 2005 but we were more fortunate to have all the television media and the majority of the print media on our side. The *Australian* has been the only blatantly negative newspaper and *The Age* and the *Sydney Morning Herald* have been strongly in our court. The *Australian* referred to us as pirates just as *The Age* once labeled the Confederate raiders as pirates. But this time *The Age* was backing us.

The one other thing that had not changed much between the visit by the *Shenandoah* and the arrival of our ships was the friendliness and the beauty of the Aussie girls.

To the Confederate sailors, the bad news from the home front was quickly forgotten with the delights of Melbourne. The ladies practically threw themselves into the arms of the rebels and Southern officers were quite talented in exercising charm, much to the annoyance of many Aussie blokes.

Thousands of visitors clamored to step onboard the Raider, and amongst them were hundreds of very pretty Aussie lasses all anxious to make the acquaintance of a Southern gentleman.

This gave rise to some fits of jealously from many of the Aussie men. In a letter to the *Herald*, one writer wrote that: "young females who go for cheap sentiment and electro-plated ware were generally anxious to defile their boots with nasty pitch this morning in order to gaze on the ultra-marine chivalry of the South…this is all very well on the part of the stupid and frivolous girls, who read sensational novels….but women have something higher and better to do in the world than to go sight-seeing in such doubtful quarters."

My officers, my crew and myself also met the wonderful ladies of Melbourne, and of Sydney, Brisbane, Cairns, Geelong, Fremantle and Hobart, and whereas the *Shenandoah* was recruiting men with great difficulty, we were able to recruit numerous men and women to join our crew. That of course would have been unthinkable in 1865. That was unfortunate for the *Shenandoah* because in my experience as the Master of the many Sea Shepherd vessels since 1979, female crew members are more hardworking, more loyal and complain less than males.

The government of Victoria immediately came under intense pressure from the American consul William Blanchard.

Blanchard, however, quickly became aware that he would not be getting much help from Governor Sir Charles Darling.

Darling was a career diplomat who previously held the position of Governor of Jamaica and Jamaica was not an easy place to govern and Darling had found that the best way to govern was to govern as little as possible. He had taken the words of Henry David Thoreau to heart that: "The government is best which governs least."

It was a stratagem that had served him well and so he specialized in the political art of doing nothing, and if doing nothing became an issue, he resorted to delegating.

Ironically but not surprisingly, this made "Do Nothing Darling" the most well-liked governor in Australian history.

Captain Waddell had sent a request to the Governor to undergo repairs and to bunker coal. He also requested permission to disembark his prisoners.

> *From Captain J.I. Waddell to His Excellency, Sir Charles H. Darling, K.C.B., Captain General and Governor-in-Chief of Victoria State.*
>
> *"Sir: I have the honour to announce to your excellency the arrival of the C.S.S. **Shenandoah**, under my command, in Port Phillip this afternoon, and also to communicate that the steamer's machinery requires repairs and that I am in want of coal.*
>
> *I desire that your excellency grant permission that I may make the necessary repairs and supply of coal to enable me to get to sea as quickly as possible.*
>
> *I desire also your excellency's permission to land my prisoners.*
>
> *I shall observe the neutrality.*
>
> *I have the honour to be, sir, your most obedient servant.*
>
> *J.I. Waddell*

Darling delayed answering for as long as possible and then informed Waddell that he could remain in port until his propeller was fixed and he was fully supplied. He then asked for a list of names of the prisoners onboard and sent a letter to Blanchard asking if the United States was prepared to take responsibility for the prisoners.

The decision over the prisoners soon became academic because within a few days of arrival, all of the prisoners had simply left the ship on their own accord.

Waddell sent a letter to James G. Francis, the commissioner of Trade and Customs stating: "In regard to a list of prisoners, I have to communicate that all those persons whom on the high seas I considered my prisoners left my ship without my knowledge, in shore boats, soon after my arrival in this port."

U.S. Consul Blanchard was able to interview the prisoners and from them learned that the *Shenandoah* was in fact the former British vessel *Sea King* and that the transfer had taken place near Madeira. Most damning was the report that the guns and ammunition on the Confederate raider had been transferred to the *Shenandoah* from the British ship *Laurel*.

With the statements from the prisoners, Blanchard believed he had all the evidence he needed to stop Waddell. It was plain to him that the *Shenandoah* was in breach of Britain's Neutrality Act.

He sent off letters to the U.S. Consulates in Hong Kong and England, although such letters would not be answered for months. He knew that stopping the Rebels in Australia would have to be his own doing, and so he dashed off a letter to Governor Darling.

As he explained it: "As soon as I had reason to believe that the *Shenandoah* and the *Sea King* were one and the same ship and that she had not entered any port since leaving England, I took the position towards authorities here that she was not entitled to any of the rights of a belligerent as contemplated in Her Majesty's neutrality proclamation, and that she could not change her nationality at sea."

Blanchard thought correctly that he had the *Shenandoah* dead to rights. There was a clear violation of the Neutrality Act and he had the evidence to prove it.

This put Governor Darling in a difficult position. If he seized the ship, it would be an admission that the law had been broken, and if he did not seize the ship, the *Shenandoah* would continue to burn and plunder American merchant ships.

Darling knew that if he seized the ship, there would be an angry outcry from the citizens of Victoria, and that if he did not seize the ship, he would anger the United States.

Darling had, however, polished his skills well and delegated the decision to a special counsel of legal advisors and then communicated to Blanchard that he would act once he received their opinion.

Darling also made sure that he was unavailable to Captain Waddell, the representative of the Confederate government, and thus by avoiding both Blanchard and Waddell he hoped to put off any decision.

As the repairs were underway, the officers and crew attended dinners, parties, and balls and also enjoyed the theatre, the horse races and romantic walks with young Victorian ladies.

"Whenever and wherever an officer appeared on shore he was forthwith surrounded by a little conclave of sympathetic admirers," wrote Cornelius Hunt. "Had we accepted a tithe of the invitations we received to indulge in spirituous comforts, we should all of us, from the Captain down to the toughest old shellbacks in the forecastle, have been shockingly inebriated during the whole period of our sojourn."

The experiences of the crew of the *Shenandoah* mirrored perfectly the experiences of my own officers and crew in our visits to Australian ports, especially so in Melbourne and Williamstown where the pubs provided free pints to anyone with a Sea Shepherd crew shirt and invitations poured in for dinners, parties, concerts and events. Metallica, the Red Hot Chili Peppers and Nickleback on their tours through Australia invited us backstage with free tickets for their concerts. The Australian surfing gear company Quiksilver partnered with Sea Shepherd on a merchandise deal. Blue Tongue Breweries delivered a $250,000 donation along with fifty cases of Blue Tongue Beer and a campaign to promote Whale

Safe Beer to illustrate that many of the brands identified as Aussie were in fact owned by Japanese companies. I was even invited to a dinner with the Governor General as a special guest of Senator Bob Brown of Tasmania.

Fremantle and Casey gave us honorary homeport status and Victoria Docklands granted us free berthage in the heart of Melbourne.

And as we were being shown such hospitality, we were also a source of concern for the Federal government in Canberra. The Japanese government was not very happy, and although Australia was taking Japan to court over their illegal whaling activities in the Southern Ocean, there were still considerable trade considerations and Japan wanted us stopped.

This placed the government between a rock and a hard place because every time they tried to appease Japan they angered our supporters.

Captain Waddell and his crew had only to ward off the bureaucrats for weeks. We made a routine of it spreading over seven years.

Waddell had also to contend with attempts by the U.S. Consulate to trick him into more blatant violations of the Neutrality Act by sending in volunteers to deceitfully join his crew by denying their British citizenship. Waddell saw through this scheme although he was in desperate need of new recruits.

There were also rumors of plans to sabotage the *Shenandoah*. A carpenter working on installing a desk in the captain's cabin informed Waddell that he had overheard some Americans discussing a plan to smuggle themselves on board with the intent to capture the raider after she put to sea.

Waddell doubled his watch and challenged every boat that approached him from the water.

The U.S. Consul did enjoy some success with his offer of $100 to any man who deserted from the *Shenandoah*. Eighteen of the crew availed themselves of the bribe and slipped over the side.

At one point, Darling was pressured by Blanchard to surround the *Shenandoah* with armed police while the ship was in drydock in Williamstown, demanding that the vessel be searched for British citizens. Waddell refused.

Melbourne's police chief Thomas Lyttleton responded by returning with a corps of fifty Royal artillery and some fifty constables armed with rifles. A tense stand-off was developing as the police took up positions surrounding the drydock.

According to Cornelius Hunt: "Captain Waddell peremptorily refused to permit his ship to be searched, or one of the Governor's men to come on board, and in doing this, he simply stood upon his rights and dignity as the commander of a cruiser, it being contrary to all precedent, to search a man-of-war for any purpose. He also wrote the Governor, informing him that if the ship was not released within twenty-four hours he should pay of his crew, return to England with his officers and report the outrage to his own and the English government."

The next day Lylttleton withdrew his men and Waddell was informed he was at liberty to proceed to sea whenever he so desired.

That very night the officers were invited to a ball in their honor at Balarat about forty miles away to which many of the officers traveled by rail.

Hunt described this affair at the Craig Hotel called the "Buccaneer's Ball" in Balarat quite happily in his book:

"It was a decidedly a recherché affair. The wealth, beauty, and fashion of Balarat were out in full force, fully intent upon lionizing and doing honour to a few of the unpretending supporters of a young government battling for existence with the lusty giant of the Western world. Every attention that kindness and courtesy could suggest was shown us, and more than one heart beat quicker at such convincing evidence of the existence of sympathy in this country of the Antpodes, for the service in which we were engaged. Many a grey uniform coat lost its gilt buttons that night, but we saw them again ere we bade a final adieu to Australia, suspended from watch guards on the necks of bright-eyed women, and we appreciated the compliment thus paid, not to us, but to our country.

"God bless the gentle women of Melbourne and Balarat! They are remembered gratefully by the officers of the renowned ship whose official history was so brief but so brilliant."

This of course is how many of my crew, including myself, remember the acquaintances we joyfully discovered ourselves, down under. And not just men meeting Aussie women but my female crew also meeting Aussie men. A few of these encounters evolved into marriages and children. For myself, I have the most pleasant of memories of one very special lady living in Queensland.

The connection to the feelings of the Confederate sailors and my own sailors of our time in Australia and our shared experiences has given me an empathy and a kinship with these men of the Southern States of the Confederacy.

On the morning of February 17th, just some three weeks after arriving in Melbourne, the *Shenandoah* loaded three hundred tons of coal from the British collier *John Frazer*, to supplement the four hundred tons already onboard.

The next morning on February 18th the Confederate raider *Shenandoah* headed out into the Bass Straits and eastward into the Tasman Sea, then northeastward towards the South Pacific islands.

CHAPTER **XIII**

A Fiery April Fool's Day Surprise

April 1, 1865
The Burning of the *Edward Carey*,
the *Pearl*, the *Hector*, and the *Harvest*

The *Shenandoah* left a very frustrated and angry U.S. Consul in its wake. Blanchard was nothing if not relentless in his efforts to stop the Confederates, but he was up against their popularity with the citizens, and a Governor who was not interested in being Lincoln's lapdog. Darling did what Darling was good at, and that was to do nothing, or to do little, or to delegate to buy time, and Waddell made good on the time he had to get well clear of Australia.

And although he lost some men to Blanchard's bribes, he was quite "surprised" that once out upon the open sea, some forty-five men appeared from the bowels of the cruiser and assembled themselves on the main deck.

Cornelius Hunt described the appearance of the men in his memoirs:

"A surprise awaited us upon getting fairly outside. Our ship's company had received a mysterious addition of forty-five men, who now made their appearance from every conceivable place where a human being could conceal himself from vigilant eyes. Fourteen of the number crept out of the bowsprit, which was of iron and hollow, where they had come very near ending their existence by suffocation; twenty more turned out of some water-tanks which were dry; another detachment was unearthed from the lower hold, and at last the whole number of stowaways were mustered forward, and word was passed to the captain to learn his pleasure concerning them.

"Personally, I felt a good deal of annoyance over the affair, as it had been my watch a part of the preceding night, and strict orders had been given to prevent any sailors from coming onboard except our own, as it were far from wishing to complicate ourselves in any way with the English government. How such a number of men could have gained our decks unseen was a mystery to me then and is still; but there they were, and the question now was, how to dispose of them.

"Captain Waddell soon made his appearance, not in the best of humor, and without any circumlocution demanded of our new recruits to what country they belonged and for what purpose they were there.

"The old sea-dogs chuckled … and with one accord protested that they were natives of the Southern Confederacy, and had come onboard thus surreptitiously for the purpose of joining us."

Although they were in truth from a dozen different nations, according to Hunt, they did demonstrate to be; "good men and true they proved, and very useful before our cruise was ended."

My own crews are international in make-up and I tend to pick up recruits in every port. On average we have between a dozen and two dozen different nationalities on every campaign, and just like the crews of the Confederate raiders, our crews were united by a shared sense of adventure and passion for a cause: their cause being the Confederacy and our cause being the whales. With respect to the whales, the cause of the Confederate raiders and the cause of my Sea Shepherd ships and crew were one and the same – to stop whaling and to cause economic ruination to the whaling industry.

As a ship's captain I find it hard to believe that Waddell and his officers were unaware of forty-five men hiding onboard their ship. The fact is that Waddell needed these men and they were not just any men. For the most part they were skilled, capable hands, and not the kind one would usually find stowing away. Critics have stated that Waddell and his officers lied about how these men

came onboard, and perhaps they did. But Waddell was well aware that deception is the foundation of strategy, and the object was to win the war. To win the war, he needed a ship and men to handle the ship, and Neutrality Act or not, he intended to replace the men that Blanchard had enticed away with bribes, an action that was also a violation of the Neutrality Act. When the Melbourne and Williamstown police refused to apprehend his deserters, this gave Waddell just cause in his mind to skirt the Act in his need for the men he required.

Two of these men most certainly were not a surprise to Waddell. The first was Captain John Blacker of the British steamer *Saxonia* that was anchored in Melbourne, close by the *Shenandoah*. He had deserted his own command to join the Confederate raider, and it is difficult to believe that Waddell did not have prior knowledge of this.

The second stowaway was said to be a genuine Confederate veteran who claimed to have been wounded at the battle of Shiloh. His name was George P. Canning, and he had "snuck" onboard with a black manservant who he insisted be paid equal wages, a request that Waddell curiously did not deny.

Canning did have a gunshot wound to his chest and was at a loss for a lung. He spoke with a Southern accent. His stories, however, did not ring true, but the best guess was that he came to Melbourne onboard the *John Frazer* and may well have been one of James Bulloch's agents in Europe. What is evident is that Waddell certainly did not treat him as a stowaway and gave him considerable respect.

Captain Waddell and his crew were not yet aware, but the might of the United States Navy was rapidly turning in their direction. But in a world of limited communications, finding a ship in the Pacific was not an easy task.

Commander C.R.P. Rodgers of the USS *Iroquois* was in Ceylon when he was notified that the *Shenandoah* was in Melbourne. He quickly realized that the Confederates would be gone by the time he reached the south of Australia, so he set sail for the Sundra Strait.

Also heading into the Pacific were the USS *Santee, Suwanee, Wachusett,* and *Wyoming.*

In truth the United States had no idea just where in the Pacific the *Shenandoah* would be. There were reports of sightings off Chile and Peru and even reports from Bermuda. Many of these reports were spread by Confederate agents to frighten American vessels from putting to sea.

In March of 1865, the United States Navy had only one target in all the seas of the world. That target was the *Shenandoah*.

Waddell was unconcerned. He now had the freedom of the sea and he had his mission. No matter how beaten down the South was, he and his crew intended to do their duty to the best of their ability, and what Waddell knew was that in the Pacific were Yankee whalers. Lots of them!

But where?

By March of 1865, the Confederate raiders had terrorized the world's oceans in their pursuit of Yankee commerce and they had been hugely successful.

Two hundred and fifty American ships were sunk and another 700 were sold into foreign ownership. The Confederacy had indeed struck the North a hard economic blow to their maritime ambitions, and this kept the British dominance firmly in first place. So despite the Neutrality Act, the Confederacy was furthering British interests as it weakened American interests, and the British were very much aware of this. Yankee ships were making themselves scarce upon the waters.

This of course goes a long way in justifying Blanchard's frustrations when he said in a bitterly worded report to President Lincoln, "There are eyes that do not see and ears that do not hear, and I fear that this port is endowed with such a portion of them as may be required to suit the occasion."

The South Pacific was empty and not a sail was spotted as they made their way north past Fiji and the Ellice Islands.

What they did encounter was a series of violent squalls lasting over four days, followed by a dead calm accompanied by unbearable humidity.

On March 20th, with his men bored and taken to stealing rum from the stores, Waddell ordered the ship to head for the Gilbert Island chain, also known as the Cannibal Islands.

Finding nothing there, they did waylay a schooner, the *Pelin* of Oahu registry, a few days later, whose Captain Hammond informed them that there might be whalers near Ascension Island. He had seen them some three weeks earlier, he said.

Waddell was hopeful, for the crew were getting restless.

It had been a full four months since the destruction of the *Edward* although the *Shenandoah* had taken the merchant ship *Delphine* on December 29 1864, before putting into Melbourne for repairs.

As dawn broke on the morning of April 1, 1865, the 2,500-foot cone of the mountain that formed Ponape Island became visible through a dense cloud of fog. By 08:00 hours the fog had been burnt off, revealing this remote island that had been known by many names including Pohnpei, John Bulls Island, Harpers Island, Sevyavin Island, William the Fourth Island, and Ascension.

Although the island was "discovered" in 1528 by the Spanish explorer Alvaro Saaveda, it was considered of little use until the whalers began stopping in to fill their water casks in the early part of the nineteenth century.

This was not good for the native inhabitants, and even less so when the missionaries landed in the wake of the whale slayers to save the souls of the people corrupted by the whalers.

The whalers brought tobacco, alcohol, and venereal disease, and the missionaries brought confusion and imposed shame and guilt.

To be fair to the missionaries, they saw their task of saving souls to be most difficult, as the Christian whalers clearly demonstrated behavior contrary to what the Christian missionaries were preaching.

The missionary brothers Luther and Theodore Gulick once wrote a letter to the owners of New England whaling ships denouncing the character of the sailors for their seduction of the native women on the island.

The letter did not mince words. "Most of the ships which you are sending to this ocean are the most disgusting of moral pesthouses. Not only are the sailors given to every crime, but the captains with nearly all their officers practice in these vices similar to those which brought destruction to Sodom and Gomorrah."

The Gulick brothers would have seen the righteousness of what would unfold that day. Four of these Yankee pesthouses were about to be cleansed by rebel fire, for the *Shenandoah* had arrived quietly that morning, dropping anchor inside the harbor.

Anchored nearby and completely oblivious to the threat that had just appeared in their midst were four whaling ships. The *Edward Carey* out of San Francisco, the *Pearl* out of New London, the *Hector* out of New Bedford, and the *Harvest* out of Honolulu. Three were proudly flying the Stars and Stripes and the fourth, although by every appearance an American whaler, flew the Hawaiian flag.

Thomas Harrocke, an Englishman, was the pilot for the island. He was an escapee from the penal colony in Australia and had been resident on the island with his native wife for some thirteen years.

One of the whaling boats had been lent to the pilot from one of the whalers, with a Yankee crew to bring him out to the newly arrived ship. The oarsmen were completely oblivious that they were helping to escort their enemy into port.

"I could scarcely conceive a more degraded looking object," Hunt had written in his journal referring to Harrocke. "He had adopted, perforce, no doubt, the habits of the Islanders; his body was tattooed with all manner of fantastic designs, and he spoke his mother tongue with hesitation and difficulty. He had married a native woman, who had borne him two children, one of whom was still living; and so far as I could learn, he was treated with kindness and consideration by the savages among whom his lot had been cast, but the torrid climate, with unnatural and perhaps oftentimes disgusting food, had made sad inroads upon a naturally robust constitution, and it was plain to see that he was descending by slow but sure stages to the grave."

Hunt added, "Thus far we had displayed no bunting and as would be naturally expected, one of the first questions our pilot asked on coming on board was in regard to our nationality."

Waddell intentionally misinformed the pilot that the ship was a Union cruiser, and the pilot agreed to take them in for thirty dollars.

Waddell, however, was very suspicious at having found such easy prey and the fact that the pilot had been ferried out by the whalers. Waddell made a show of belting a pistol around his waist and informing a very confused Harrocke that he would be shot if there was a hint of trickery. Waddell was well aware that if Harrocke was a Union supporter and suspected the true identify of the ship, he could easily put the vessel on the rocks.

The whalers had told Harrocke that the ship appeared to be American and possibly engaged in the survey of the islands.

Harrocke proved to be a colorful character and gleefully entertained the officers with yarns about his adventures on the island for the hour it took to bring the large ship into an anchorage about a mile distant from the four whalers.

As soon as the anchor was dropped and held secure at a place close to shore and hawsers run to stout trees on the beach to prevent her swinging, four boats were lowered, each manned with sailors carrying sidearms. Each boat carried two officers armed with Colt .45 revolvers. As they shoved off towards the whaling vessels, a blank shot was fired and the Confederate flag was run up the mast.

The pilot Harrocke stood open mouthed as he watched. According to Hunt, he "stood for a few moments watching the receding boats, then turned his eyes aloft, curiously scanning the, to him, strange bunting that streamed out in the breeze, and finally, turning to the officer on deck, he asked what flag that was, why we had fired the gun, and why those boats, filled with armed men, were putting off towards the whalers."

"All answered in a word, my hearty," replied the officer addressed. "Those four ships are prizes to the Confederate government."

"And what the hell is the Confederate government?" replied the old pilot in astonishment.

"The best and biggest part of what was the United States of America. The Yankees didn't sail the government ship to suit us, so we cut adrift and started on our own hook."

"The hell! What are you going to do with your prizes?"

"Set them on fire bye and bye, after we have taken what we want out of them."

"Well, you and the Yankees must settle that business to suit yourselves. If I had known what you were up to, maybe I should not have piloted you in, for I don't like to see a bonfire made of a good ship."

The American whalers were also shocked at the morning's turn of events. The first and second officers were brought on board the **Shenandoah**. The four captains had been on shore after a night of indulgence amongst the natives. Waddell ordered a boat to be kept on stand-by to watch for the return of the four skippers.

Around 17:00 hours, a boat was seen coming from shore and the Yankee officers reported that these were the four captains. The boat had not gone far before it stopped with the men resting on the oars as they made out the Confederate flag, and realizing their predicament, turned about and headed back to the beach. They were quickly overtaken and brought back to the raider, where they found their officers and crews shackled in irons.

The masters of the **Edward Carey, Pearl,** and **Hector** could not protest, as they had displayed the American flag and their papers identified them as such. The **Harvest** out of Oahu would have been exempt, except that her captain and mates were American, her ownership was American, the captain could not produce a bill of sale to a Honolution, and her previous port of registry was New Bedford. Flying the Hawaiian flag was not going to save her from the torch.

Realizing that their ships and their cargoes of oil were to be destroyed, the whalers became angry, forcing Waddell for the first time to confine the masters to irons along with the crew.

Of the 130 whalers, he recruited only seven for his crew. Four were Portuguese, two were Yankees, and one was an African American. Most of the whalers were Hawaiians, and they elected to stay on the island.

The more the Confederates were exposed to whalers, the more they were beginning to hold them in contempt. Waddell described the crew of the four vessels as, "timid… easily imposed upon and cheated but suiting the purpose of such men as command whalers."

The four whalers were not as rich in provisions as the *Edward* but still provided a bounty of satisfying goods. The Confederates did seize some valuable items including two sextants, six quadrants, and eight chronometers. In addition, they found two dozen United States infantry uniforms that were easily converted to Confederate marine uniforms.

The greatest prize of all was the discovery of a large number of up-to-date specialized charts outlining the movements of the whales, and thus of the whalers. Waddell noted the chart "to show every track they make where they have been most successful in taking whales."

These four ships provided Waddell with a treasure of great value to their objectives. He now had in his possession the charts of the whaling grounds of the Bering and Okhotsk Seas.

In the vast area of the Pacific and Arctic oceans, finding whalers, as I have learned myself, is like finding a needle in a haystack; and without a reliable intelligence source, while not impossible, it is exceedingly difficult. Waddell had found the *Edward* and the four ships at Ascension by stumbling accidently upon them, but now he had a key to hunting the Yankee whale slayers down.

Although I had much success in tracking whalers in the North Atlantic and North Pacific, my 2002/2003 voyage to the Southern Ocean yielded not a single sighting of a Japanese whaler. After four months of searching I knew that I would not be able to return until I found a way to determine locations and movements; and thus, it was not until 2005 that I was able to do so.

After removing all the goods they wanted from the four ships, Waddell invited the King to have his people take whatever they wanted before he burned them.

Cornelius Hunt observed, "After securing what we desired from the prizes, and giving the officers and men an opportunity of procuring such personal effects as they desired to save, the natives were allowed to go onboard and ransack the doomed vessels to their heart's content. Such an occasion for wholesale plundering had never occurred before, and was not likely to again, and they made the most of it. All day long they swarmed over the vessels, like driver ants upon a dead carcass, and their canoes were constantly passing to and fro, laden with ship's bread, tobacco, bits of iron, harpoons and whaling lines, and all sorts of odds and ends, until they were fairly surfeited with plundering."

During the evening of April 3rd, Lieutenant Sidney Smith Lee Jr., on orders from Captain Waddell, commenced with the destruction of the first of the four whalers. He set fire to the *Pearl*.

In short order John Grimball set fire to the *Edward Carey* and Francis Chew ignited the *Hector*. Their details first weighed the anchors of the two vessels, allowing them to drift onto a shoal a safe distance from the shore. There the two vessels were torched, and the resulting conflagration was a spectacle indeed, one of great joy for the Confederates, of anger and sadness from the whalers, and awe and confusion from the natives.

Lieutenant Chew wrote in his journal what the whalers were most likely feeling. "What a destruction of property, obtained by so much toil and hardships!"

The five hundred barrels of oil on the three ships caused the vessels to burn magnificently for three days and nights, and such a bonfire, the natives could not comprehend. According to Hunt the natives stood on the shore "wildly gesticulating why all this wealth should be thus ruthlessly destroyed."

It was a grand crematorium for the hundreds of whales slain by the Yankee whalers whose oil had been secured through a remorseless cruelty. The whalers may not have had one ounce of compassion in their hardened hearts for their innocent victims, but many wept that day to see the fruits of their long labors billow skyward in a dense cloud of inky black smoke. Finally a degree of punishment had befallen these heartless men not just for the deaths of the whales, but also for their many misdeeds against the natives.

The crew of the *Shenandoah* were given five days of liberty to explore the islands for rest and recreation. They spent the time getting tattoos, fishing, and swimming, all of them both satisfied and happy with the progress of their voyages. They had captured twelve Yankee vessels, destroying ten of them, five of which were whalers, and they now had the key to tracking down and destroying the entire Pacific and Arctic whaling fleets.

Unfortunately, the April Fool's Day joke was also on them.

April 10th, the last day on the island before they put out to sea to head north, was not an especially auspicious day for the crew of the *Shenandoah,* despite their high spirits.

April 10th on the Micronesian side of the International Date Line meant it was April 9, 1865 in Appomattox, Virginia, where General Robert E. Lee rode up to the courthouse and sat down across the desk from General Ulysses S. Grant and surrendered.

The Confederate States of America had lost the war and the Confederacy had ceased to exist.

Fortunately for the whales, Captain James I. Waddell would not know of the defeat of his country until August 2, 1865, after which time twenty-one more whalers would be destroyed. The four whalers at Popane Island were the last Yankee ships legally destroyed in the Civil War.

On the eve of reconstruction, the war was all but over except for an actor named John Wilkes Booth and a small crew of sailors on the far side of the world.

Although they did not know it and would not know it for three months, the *Shenandoah* was now a pirate.

On the 13th of April at precisely 15:00 hours, Irvine Bulloch made an entry to the ship's log: "Speed eight knots, wind at force four, the barometer holding steady at 29.87."

Three in the afternoon in Micronesia was 22:00 hours in Washington D.C. and the exact moment that John Wilkes Booth stepped into the Presidential box at the Ford Theater while Abraham Lincoln was watching a performance of *Our American Cousin.* As Bullock touched his pen to the page in the logbook, Booth fired a fatal bullet into the back of the President's head.

Booth's shot was not the last shot of the war, however, for the *Shenandoah* would have that honor in the weeks to come.

The war to win victory and glory for the Confederacy was over, but the war to save the lives of hundreds of whales and in all likelihood the salvation of a species would continue.

Waddell had the charts from the whalers he had destroyed at Ascension Island in his possession, and those charts pointed the way northward to the Bering Sea and beyond.

Waddell wrote in his memoirs that: "With such charts in my possession, I not only held a key to the navigation of all the Pacific Islands, the Okhotsk and Bering Seas, and the Arctic Ocean, but the most probable localities for finding the great Arctic whaling fleet of New England, without a tiresome search."

The *Shenandoah* would bring the Civil War to the one place it had not yet come, and that was the waters between Russian and Alaska. There he knew he would find the whalers and once found, he would put the greasy floating abattoirs to the torch.

Strangely enough, with the demise of the Confederacy, the triumph of the *Shenandoah* over the whalers was in the ascendancy. This Confederate raider would soon inflict more damage to the Yankee whaling fleet after the surrender at Appomattox than before.

Chapter IV

The Sea of Okhotsk

May 20–June 13 1865

The last thing that Captain Ebenezer Nye expected to show up for lunch at noon on May 27, 1865, was a Confederate raider.

His ship the *Abigail* was 33 months out of New Bedford and he was back in the Sea of Okhotsk after unloading a cargo of whale oil in Japan, where he had purchased several silk dresses and exquisitely crafted lacquer boxes to eventually take home.

Nye was an unscrupulous trader and opportunist. He had only 20 barrels of whale oil onboard. By contrast he had much more alcohol on board than whale oil - 736 gallons of cheap whiskey, 462 gallons of gin, eight barrels of rum and one barrel of pure alcohol. All for trading with Siberian natives for furs. In addition, he had 700 bottles of brandy and an excessively large supply of champagne, wine and schnapps.

It was around noon when he noticed a large black ship on the other side of a broken-up floe of ice. He was not alarmed, in fact he was elated. The large ship hoisted the Imperial Russian flag and Nye saw an opportunity for some friendly banter and trade.

Nye's brother back in New Bedford owned a distillery, and Russians like to drink.

On the *Shenandoah*, the officers smiled as the *Abigail* hoisted the Stars and Stripes and instead of fleeing, the old whaler worked her way around the floe to meet up with the ship. The furthest thing from his mind was danger. The last thing he was expecting was a run-in with the Confederate rebels.

As he came alongside, his crew were cheering until they were shocked to see the Russian flag quickly lowered and replaced by the white Confederate ensign.

Within minutes officers Dabney Scales and Joshua Minor boarded the whaler to take possession and to relieve her skipper of his command.

Nye's face grew pale as he tried to stifle his anger. His Yankee stoicism took over and he scratched his head and said, "Well, I s'pose I'm taken! But who on earth would have thought of seeing one of your Southern privateers up here in the Okhotsk Sea. I heard of some of your pranks you fellows have been playing, but I supposed I was out of your reach."

Scales replied, "Why the fact of the business is, Captain, we have entered into a treaty offensive and defensive with the whales and are up here by special agreement to disperse their mortal enemies."

There has been some dispute about who actually said this. The Boarding officers were Dabney Scales and Joshua Minor. Some accounts state that it was Minor who made this statement. The confusion has resulted because Master's Mate Cornelius Hunt did not mention which officer made the remark in his accounting of the incident. I'm inclined to attribute the quote to Scales based on what I've read about his personality and the fact that he had a wry sense of humor. In his book *The Lost Fleet*, Marc Songini states that it was Cornelius Hunt who said this, but Hunt's own account stated that he did not board the *Abigail*.

Captain Nye replied to this with resignation. "All right. I never grumble at anything I can't help, but the whales don't owe me much of a grudge. Lord knows I haven't disturbed them much this voyage, though I've done my part at blubber-hunting in years gone by."

Aside from the whales, Nye was getting a righteous punishment for the misery and death he had inflicted on the Inuit and Yupik peoples.

During the nineteenth century, everywhere on the world's oceans that whalers ventured they spread disease, violence and misery.

In 1826, a whaling ship drained water barrels into a stream on Maui so they could refill the casks with fresh clean water. The water they dumped was filled with mosquito larvae.

There was not a single mosquito in Hawaii until this reckless act in 1826 by whalers. What followed was the extinction of half of Hawaii's birds from Avian malaria.

In the far north, hundreds of thousands of animals were slaughtered for their fur to be bartered away with alcohol and tobacco.

Conservationist John Muir once wrote: "To the Eskimo it is misery and often times quick death." Muir personally witnessed native people who starved to death or killed each other under the influence of alcohol.

Nye's liquor almost cost Waddell his own command on the *Shenandoah* when his crew and some officers discovered this huge stash of booze. Many of them, including Dabney Scales, were placed in irons and gagged.

Thirty hours after being boarded, the *Abigail* was set afire after being relieved of prizes like silk dresses, lacquer boxes, a chronometer, and some 25 barrels of booze. The ship burned brilliantly surrounded by ice against the white background of the mountains.

Nye did not do badly, however. He was part owner of the boat, which was insured, and the cargo he had unloaded in Japan was worth many times what he lost on that fateful day.

On June 3rd, Captain Waddell, in full uniform, entered the officer's mess with several bottles of the recently liberated champagne. The occasion was Jefferson Davis's 57th birthday.

It was also 57 days since the surrender of the Confederacy and yet less than a week earlier, a Yankee whaler was burned by their rebellious hands.

Of course, they still had no way of knowing the war was over or that the South had lost. In the eyes of the North they would be simply pirates.

Fortunately for the whales, they remained oblivious of the state of affairs back in the beleaguered Southern States.

The crew of the *Abigail* were exceedingly helpful. After expressing his disappointment at not finding any more whalers in the Sea of Okhotsk, a number of the *Abigail's* crew signed onto the *Shenandoah* and eagerly provided the information that the *Shenandoah* needed – the coordinates for the great Arctic fleet of whalers.

CHAPTER XV

A Glorious Destruction

T he sea of Okhotsk was a misery filled with long days of fog and worrisome ice conditions. They only had one prize to show for all their wearisome efforts, the unfortunate *Abigail*.

The voyage did yield exciting fruit with the complicity of the *Abigail's* crew who eagerly supplied Waddell with the coordinates for the New England Arctic fleet.

Lieutenant Francis Chew wrote of how excited he was to be heading northward to this "great whaling ground."

"They go to hunt the whales," said Chew, "and we go to hunt the whalers."

With that information, the *Shenandoah* moved slowly southward through dense fog and threatening ice towards the Amphitrite Strait. The June breakup was pushing huge chunks of rotten ice all around them, making the voyage dangerously difficult.

Finally, on June 14th, the *Shenandoah* slipped under the Kamchatka Peninsula and set a course northward to the Bering Sea. Some 1600 miles ahead lay the greatest prize of all – the great Yankee Bowhead whaling fleet.

Waddell was so confident of success that he ordered the complete clearing out of all the 'tween deck space in anticipation of hundreds of prisoners.

Thousands of miles to the southeast the rebels had disarmed, Lincoln was dead and their President Jefferson Davis was an inmate in Fortress Monroe on the coast of Virginia.

Completely oblivious to these facts, the crew of the *Shenandoah* headed northward with the intent of mass destruction to the Yankee whaling fleet.

On June 21st, the longest day of the year, the crew saw clear signs of whaling activity. Pieces of blubber and long pinkish intestines.

Lieutenant Whittle reckoned that with a northeast current, the whalers should lie to the southwest of the Shenandoah's current position. They set a course towards the source of the floating gore.

On June 22nd, the first whaler was sighted about eighteen miles off Cape Thaddeus. There was no mistaking it for anything but a whale killer with thick black smoke rising from the trypots, clearly indicating that the ship was in the process of rendering a whale.

The *Shenandoah* raised the Russian flag and moved closer without arousing any suspicion or alarm. When both ships were in cannon range, the Russian flag was brought down and speedily replaced by the Southern ensign.

It was the *William Thompson* with a large Bowhead whale strapped alongside, the largest ship in the entire New England whaling fleet.

Lieutenant Whittle noted in his logbook:

"At 9:00 A.M. we made two sails on our port quarter. Furled sails and stood for them under steam. At 11:00 hove to and boarded the six topsail yards whale ship *William Thompson* of New Bedford. Mass., Capt. Smith. Put a prize crew onboard & brought the captain and mates aboard our vessel and stood in chase for the other vessel."

As the *Shenandoah* boarding party were climbing the ladder to the whaler's deck, the lookout on the Raider spied a 2nd ship. Waddell dropped off a prize crew and immediately made way for the second ship, the *Euphrates*.

The *Euphrates* continued to regard the *Shenandoah* as a Russia ship and made no effort to escape. The Confederate crew boarded the whaler, removed the crew and quickly plundered the vessel of stores before knocking out bulkheads and opening oil barrels before setting the ship on fire only a few hours after capture.

As the fire burned, the *Shenandoah* returned to the *William Thompson* to begin the work of transferring water and stores.

As Captain Francis Smith of the *William Thompson* prepared to present his papers to Captain Waddell, the first mate of the whaler angrily confronted Orris Browne, the leader of the prize crew.

'My God, man, don't you know the war has ended?'

"Did Grant surrender?"

"No, the army of Virginia surrendered. The war is over."

"Sir, the war will not be over until the South is free."

The plundering of the *William Thompson* was interrupted by the cry of "sail ho."

"Where away?"

"Five points off the port bow and standing north."

Leaving the small boats behind with the whaler, the *Shenandoah* raised steam and sail and set off on their third pursuit of the day.

Catching up with it, Lieutenant Whittle boarded the *Robert Townes* and to his disappointment discovered it was the out of Sydney, Australia, and that nation's only whaling ship.

The Confederates turned back, passing the still burning *Euphrates* to resume the work of removing stores. At 03:00 hours, the *William Thompson* was set on fire

Waddell and his crew then proceeded to the northeast, crossing the dateline into the same day of June 22nd. Moving through dense fog and snow squalls, the *Shenandoah* moved onward until with the lifting of the fog around noon, a very welcome sight met their eyes with the spotting of five sails on the other side of a large floe of ice.

Flying the Russian flag, the black ship worked her way around the floes as more sails came into view. By 16:00 hours there were eight ships in sight.

A whaling operation was underway and the crew saw a whale boat swiftly moving across the water, towed by a large Bowhead whale. Nearby was their mother ship, the *Milo* out of New Bedford.

It was the *Milo's* lucky day. Waddell needed to offload prisoners from the *Abigail*, the *William Thompson* and the *Euphrates*. He bonded the whaler for $46,000 and transferred the captured whaling crews.

As the negotiations with the captain of the *Milo* were underway, two more sails were spotted. The wind was picking up and one of the vessels headed into the ice while the other made a run for the Siberian shore hoping to reach neutral Russian waters. Captain Moses Tucker onboard the 426-ton *Sophia Thornton* judged that his ice strengthened vessel could lose the *Shenandoah* in the thick floes.

Waddell fired a 32-pound shot from his Whitworth gun that came very close to the whaler's figurehead. Captain Tucker was not deterred as he kept pushing into thicker ice. The *Shenandoah* fired a second shot that ripped through the main topsail forcing Captain Tucker to turn about and work his way back out of the ice.

Waddell did not have much time to speak with Captain Tucker. He had the captain, his officers and crew locked into the forward coal bunker and immediately turned to hunt down the second fleeing ship, hoping to catch her before reaching Russian waters.

The 428-ton *Jireh Swift* almost made it to Siberian waters. Unfortunately for Captain Thomas Williams, the wind changed, allowing the *Shenandoah* under steam to catch up. Within 30 minutes of her capture, the *Jireh Swift* was in flames.

The *Shenandoah* returned to the *Milo* and the *Sophia Thornton*. He had his carpenters cut down the masts and spars after which he instructed the crew of the *Sophia Thornton* to return, collect their possessions and set fire to their own ship. The *Milo* stood by to board the prisoners and prepared to set a course to San Francisco.

Waddell did not want to waste any time. He had spied four more sails and set off in pursuit. Looking back he saw the smoke and was satisfied that his orders had been carried out.

He brought the *Susan Abigail* to heel, approaching her with the Stars and Stripes flying. The captain of the *Susan Abigail* happily boarded the *Shenandoah*. He was fresh out of San Francisco and knew for certain that the war was over. He also had newspapers reporting the surrender by General Robert E. Lee.

Unfortunately for the captain of the *Susan Abigail*, one of the newspapers erroneously reported that Lee had eluded Federal forces and had regrouped with General E. Johnston to continue the fight. The report also claimed that President Davis had issued a new proclamation stating that the war would be carried on with renewed vigor and exhorting the people of the South to bear up heroically.

The news troubled Waddell, but he insisted that Yankee newspapers were not reliable. Lieutenant Whittle, after reading the newspapers, did not doubt the reality that the South had lost. He wrote that, "the news is, if true, very bad, but "there's life in the old land yet.' Let us live with a hope.' The God of Jacob is our refuge.' Oh, let us trust in him."

The "proof" that Captain Redfield of the *Susan Abigail* provided was insufficient to save his ship.

The *Susan Abigail* was not a whaler but she was something just as bad. She was a fur trader, bartering cheap goods including alcohol to Siberian natives for sable, fox and sea otters.

Redfield, clad in an extravagant fur coat, pleaded with Waddell but to no avail. The vessel was put to the torch, and Redfield and his crew transferred to the *Shenandoah.*

The campaign was operating on borrowed time. Captain Waddell could only keep the reality at bay for a little more time. But until then there were still whalers to be found and sunk.

In August 1981, I took my ship the *Sea Shepherd II* across from Nome, Alaska, to the coast of Siberia, passing both Little and Big Diomede islands, visible on our starboard side. Our objective was to gather evidence of illegal Soviet whaling activities, and I took a small boat ashore with two crew members, Eric Swartz and Bob Osborn, to the beach near the Siberian village of Lorino.

There were two Red Army soldiers standing on the beach when we landed, but they simply ignored us. We were wearing orange Mustang suits, and our ship, about a mile offshore, was flying the British Red Ensign, which from this distance could easily be mistaken for the Soviet flag.

For forty-five minutes we filmed and photographed what we discovered – a whaling station and above on the cliffs, holding cages for sable and fox.

We knew that the Soviets were killing whales under the guise of aboriginal subsistence needs, and now we had the proof. Rather than supplying native Siberians with food, the operation was designed to provide cheap meat for the fur industry, and because sable was highly guarded by the Soviet monopoly, hence the guards.

Fortunately for us, the guards had mistaken us for Soviet scientists. Why else would we have brazenly landed with cameras and boldly walked up to the whaling station like we had every right to do so?

We were the first to invade the Soviet Union since the end of World War II, and our invasion was a success. With the evidence in hand, we returned to our Zodiac RIB on the beach. Eric Swartz and Robert Osborne got into the boat and I began to push it out when one of the soldiers approached and calmly said, "*sto eta?*"

Still pushing the boat out, I replied, "*eta Zodiac.*"

The soldier, looking confused, now answered, "*eta Mercury.*"

That's when the realization came to me that we could not bluff this adventure for much longer. Mercury outboard motors were most likely not that common in Siberia.

Waist deep in the water, I pulled myself over the bow into the boat and softly asked, "What is he doing?"

Eric and Bob were still waving and smiling. Eric said, "He's taking his rifle off his shoulder."

I again softly said, "Smile and wave."

This confused the soldier, and he turned and began running up the beach towards the town and we presumed he was going for help.

We returned safely to the ship and began to cruise southward down the coast of Siberia.

About 45 minutes later, two dark green helicopter gunships approached with large red stars on each side. They flew around the *Sea Shepherd II* and I ignored them. One of the helicopters began to fire flares across our bow and I continued to ignore them.

A half hour later, we saw a large military ship approaching and it did not take long for it to come alongside. It was a Soviet Frigate.

It was at this point that I changed course towards St. Lawrence Island while continuing to ignore the frigate.

We were a strange site. An old British trawler flying the British Ensign but from our mast we flew the United Nations flag and the flags representing the nationalities of our crew – American, Canadian, Italian, French, German, Australian and Scotland.

The frigate raised signal flags ordering us to stop.

I ignored them.

Finally, a loud voice with a deep Russian accent came over the radio. "Sea Shepherd, Sea Shepherd, stoppa your engines. Prepare to be boarded by the Soviet Union."

One of my crew pleaded with me to stop. "Hell no, I have no intention of being locked up in Siberia."

I picked up the transmitter and replied, "This is the Sea Shepherd. I have no intention of stopping. We don't have room for the Soviet Union."

The Russian captain was not expecting a reply of "no."

Both ships continued to speed eastward with two helicopters overhead. A Soviet crew ran forward to pull the green tarps off the forward deck gun when suddenly a grey whale surfaced between both of our ships and blew a mist that the noonday sun transformed into a shower of rainbows.

A few moments later the frigate stopped the pursuit, and my first officer Neil Sanderson, standing at the chart table, announced that we were back in U.S. waters. Shortly thereafter we anchored just off of Gamble, St. Lawrence Island.

On June 25th, 116 years earlier, the *Shenandoah* was in this very spot and I was looking at the same gloomy grey volcanic island some forty miles off the Siberia coast.

Going ashore I spoke with many of the Yupik whose great grandfathers had traded with the whalers and the *Shenandoah* crew.

The *Shenandoah* departed from St. Lawrence island in pursuit of two sails. The pursuit was fruitless; the first ship was Hawaiian and the second vessel was French. Waddell decided to head northward towards the Bering Strait, and within a few hours, he captured the whaler *General Williams* out of New London.

As the *General Williams* was put to the torch, Waddell spotted three more sails to the north on the other side of a large floe of ice. The *Shenandoah* cautiously made way through the ice and reached the stern of the whaler at 01:00 hours on the 26th of June. It was the *William C. Nye* out of San Francisco.

No sooner were the prisoners of the *Nye* onboard the *Shenandoah,* the lookout spotted five more sails on the horizon. Waddell immediately set out in pursuit, using steam.

The whalers did not make any move to escape. They were becalmed and helpless on that dreary freezing sea.

It was not long before the raider came alongside the *Catherine* with a Bowhead whale lashed alongside. The whaler was now as helpless as their latest victim. Half an hour later the *Catherine* became the blazing funeral pyre for the hapless whale as the *Shenandoah* leisurely moved on towards a third becalmed vessel.

It was the New Bedford Bark *Nimrod,* and her captain James Clark was a very unhappy man. When boarding officer Smith Lee came over the side, Captain Clark recognized him as the same boarding officer from the Alabama that had taken his ship the *Ocean Rover*.

"My God, no!" he shouted as Lee came over the side.

"We meet again, Captain," Lee replied.

This whaler, named after the biblical hunter Nimrod, was quickly evacuated and set ablaze. She had barrels of whale oil from seven Bowheads to feed the flames.

These three whaling barks were all aflame at the same time and it was an incredibly dramatic spectacle for rebels and whalers alike, although with vastly different emotions separating the two parties.

By the end of the day, the *Shenandoah* had taken on some 200 prisoners and Captain Waddell had some legitimate concerns about security. He tossed the Mates and Masters into the coal hole and sent the crew onboard twelve small whaleboats they had commandeered. These twelve boats were taken under tow by the *Shenandoah.*

Cornelius Hunt wrote: "It was a singular scene upon which we now looked out. Behind us were three blazing ships, wildly drifting amid gigantic fragments of ice; close astern were the twelve whale-boats with their living freight; and ahead of us were five other vessels now evidently aware of their danger but seeing no venue for escape."

The fourth whaler taken that day was the **General Pike**. Wad-dell ransomed the ship and informed her captain that he would place 222 prisoners on board. He then made a beeline for the bark *Isabella* where he ordered her crew taken onboard the *Shenandoah*.

The day was not yet over. The bark *Gipsey* was easily overtaken and forfeited to the fortunes of war.

The break of dawn on Wednesday, June 28, 1865 began the most fiery day of destruction in the history of the Yankee whaling fleet.

At 06:30 hours, some twelve miles southwest of the Diomede Islands, the lookouts on the *Shenandoah* bellowed from the topsails, "Ten sails sighted."

Getting up steam, it took just ninety minutes to run the first whaler down, the barque **Waverly** out of New Bedford. The ship was sacked and set afire. The crew were allowed only a few minutes to gather their personal belongings.

As the smoke curled up into the clear sky, every whale in sight knew there would be no escape. Ten whaling crews stared at the oncoming black ship cutting quickly through the water without sails.

At 13:30 hours, the *Shenandoah* was amongst them. All the ships were at anchor, and nine of the ten were flying the stars and stripes.

Nine of the ships had come to the aid of the tenth. The barque **Brunswick** had been holed by ice the night before. Their kindness in responding brought them together and unfortunately sealed their fate. The *Shenandoah* was a wolf within a pack of sheep. There would be no escape, although as it turned out, there was some mercy.

Fred Chew discovered on boarding the **James Maury** that she had lost her captain during the voyage. He was met at the rail by Mrs. Gray, the late captain's wife. The lady was frightened and begged Chew not to destroy her ship. Chew assured her that no harm would befall her or her ship.

The acting captain of the *James Maury* was ordered to board the *Shenandoah* to meet with Captain Waddell. Waddell had him sign a ransom note for $37,000 and sent him back with a message for Mrs. Gray. In his notes, Waddell said that he told her that no harm should come to her the vessel; that I knew she was the owner of the vessel, and that the men of the South never made war on helpless women and children; although an example to the contrary had been set by their Northern enemy, we preferred the nobler instincts of human nature."

With the *James Maury* bonded, there was only one other obstacle from that doomed fleet. It was the *Favourite*. She was the only captive vessel that refused to lower the Stars and Stripes. Her old captain stood beside a harpoon gun with a cutlass in his hand, defying the boarding party.

"Who are you and what do you want?" he bellowed.

"We come to inform you that your vessel is a prize to the Confederate steamer *Shenandoah*."

"I'll be damned if she is, at least not just yet. Now keep off, you, or I'll fire into you."

The *Shenandoah* steamed over to where the argument was taking place.

"Haul down your flag," Grimball yelled over from the raider.

"Haul it down yourself, damn you, if you think it will be good for your constitution."

"If you don't haul it down, we'll blow you out of the water in five minutes."

"Blow away, my buck, but I may be eternally blasted if I haul down that flag for any cussed Confederate pirate that ever floated."

This was all too much for the crew of the *Favourite*. They threw down their weapons and lowered their boats, leaving their captain to defend the ship by himself.

This did not deter Captain Thomas Young, as he tossed aside his cutlass and held up a bottle of whiskey and stood by his harpoon gun.

Lieutenant Whittle brought his boat alongside and demanded that Young strike his colors.

"I'll see you dead first," Young yelled back.

"If you don't, I'll have to shoot you." Whittle raised his rifle.

Young sneered and said, "Shoot and be damned."

The Confederates stormed overboard and quickly relieved Captain Young of his bottle and of his command.

Eight ships were set afire watched by the survivors on the *James Maury* and the *Nile* and the crew of the *Shenandoah*.

No one had ever witnessed such a horrific sight.

Cornelius Hunt described the scene that day in his notes:

"We hauled off to a little distance and anchored with a kedge, to watch the mighty conflagration our hands had lighted.

"It was a scene never to be forgotten by any who beheld it. The red glare from the eight burning vessels shone far and wide over the drifting ice of these savage seas; the crackling of the fire as it made its devouring way through each doomed ship, filling the air like upbraiding voices. The sea was filled with boats driving hither and thither, with no hands to guide them, and with yards, sails, cordage, remnants of the stupendous ruin there progressing. In the distance, but where the light fell strong and red upon them, bringing out into bold relief each spar and line, were the two ransomed vessels, the Noah's Arks that were to bear away the human life which in a few hours would be all that was left of the gallant whaling fleet.

"Imagination assisted us no doubt, but we fancied we could see the varied expressions of anger, disappointment, fear, or wonder, that marked the faces of the multitude on these decks, as their eyes rested on this last great holocaust; and when, one by one, the burning hulks went hissing and gurgling down into the treacherous bosom of the ocean, the last act in the bloody drama of the American Civil War had been played."

I like to imagine that the eyes of some whales were on this burning scene, watching the destruction of their tormentors, and I often wonder just how many whales were spared the deadly harpoons because of this lonely Confederate raider.

That was the last resistance and the last inferno. Although the *Shenandoah* pushed northward into the Arctic, it became quickly evident that the ship was no match for the ice. They had seen what it had done to the ice-strengthened **Brunswick**. Waddell gave the order to turn the ship around and to head south.

For the crew of the **Shenandoah**, the war was finally over. Unfortunately, their voyage was not, and now the hunter would become the hunted. The Yankees wanted their revenge.

The situation for the captain and the crew of the **Shenandoah** was daunting. They were on the far side of the world from their home. The war had ended two months before they had laid waste to the Bering Sea whaling fleet. It would not take long for word to reach the United States, and the word of the **Shenandoah's** depredations would ignite a national firestorm of anger and condemnation.

There was no doubt in Captain Waddell's mind that the entire United States Navy would begin to hunt them down.

Robert E. Lee surrendered the last major Confederate army to Ulysses S. Grant at Appomattox Courthouse on April 9, 1865. It could be argued that the war actually ended with the last official battle at Palmito Ranch, Texas, on May 13, 1865. Even so, the **Shenandoah** had burned 21 ships and bonded four others, causing catastrophic losses for the Northern whaling industry well after May 13th.

The realization came to all hands that they were now, for all intents and purposes, to be considered criminals and pirates. There would be no safe place for them.

A decision had to be made. There really were just three choices. Surrender to the nearest United States warship or port, surrender the ship in a neutral port or surrender the ship to the British government.

After much debate and animosities, the decision was made by the captain and the officers to set to sea and the Mersey River.

CHAPTER XVI

The Last Flag Down

The *Shenandoah* headed southward towards Cape Horn. The ship was spared a thrashing as it rounded the Horn but ran into a Northeasterly gale that blew them south to the icebergs of the South Atlantic. As they worked their way through the weather northward, the decision was to avoid Cape Town and to strike for Liverpool, a decision that provoked a great deal of anger by the contingent that favored South Africa.

Fortunately, they made the right choice. The **USS Iroquois** and the USS **Wyoming** had been stationed off the Cape of Good Hope since August 8th for the sole purpose of apprehending the *Shenandoah.*

It took 122 days to sail from the Aleutians to St. George's Channel where they arrived on November 5th, covering a distance of twenty-three thousand nautical miles. During that time they had not once sighted land or communicated with another vessel.

When they reached the mouth of the Mersey River, Waddell fired a rocket to request a pilot.

It was just after midnight that the pilot boat came alongside.

"Good morning to you," the pilot said. "What ship is this?"

"The late Confederate steamer *Shenandoah*." replied Waddell.

"The deuce it is! Where have you fellows come from?"

"The Arctic Ocean."

"Have you stopped at any port since you left there?"

"No, nor been in sight of land, either. What news of the war in America?"

"It's been so long people have got through talking about it. Jeff Davis is in Fortress Monroe, and the Yankees have had a lot of cruisers out looking for you."

Proceeding up the Mersey, the *Shenandoah* was briefly grounded on a bar but refloated with the tide. The ship continued on through a foggy morning and finally dropped anchor behind the HMS *Donegal*.

Shortly thereafter, a contingent of British marines boarded the *Shenandoah* and a lieutenant officially informed the captain, the officers and the crew of the Confederate raider that the war was over.

The Confederate ensign was raised for the last time. With mixed emotions, the crew stood at attention as the colors were lowered for the last time.

Captain Waddell had tears in his eyes. It was the only Confederate flag to have circumnavigated the globe. It had flown for a full six months after the war had ended. It had covered a voyage of fifty-eight thousand nautical miles and overseen the capture of thirty-eight Yankee ships, burning thirty of them, scuttling two and bonding the remaining six. She had captured over 1,000 prisoners and had taken the war to the Bering Sea and the Arctic Ocean in pursuit of the Yankee whaling fleet. Twenty-nine of the ships she captured were taken after the official end of the war.

The last hostile shot of the American Civil War had been fired from her deck on June 22, 1865, twenty-four thousand miles away in the Arctic Ocean. It was a warning shot.

The most remarkable part of the *Shenandoah* voyage was that not a single sailor was lost to hostile fire and not a single person was injured or killed by the Confederate raider.

Captain Waddell quietly said, "I claim for my officers and men a triumph over their enemies and over every obstacle. And for myself I claim having done my duty."

Shortly thereafter, a contingent of British marines boarded the *Shenandoah* and a lieutenant officially informed the captain, the officers and the crew of the Confederate raider that the war was over.

That day, Waddell sent the following letter to Lord Russell:

Shenandoah
November 6th, 1865

My Lord,

I have the honour to announce to your lordship my arrival in the waters of the Mersey with this vessel, late a ship of war under my command, belonging to the Confederate States of America.

The singular position in which I find myself placed and the absence of all precedents on the subject will, I trust, induce your lordship to pardon my hasty reference to a few facts connected with the cruise lately made by this ship.

I commissioned the ship in October, 1864, under orders from the naval department of the Confederate States, and in pursuance of the same commenced actively raiding the enemy's commerce. My orders directed me to visit certain seas in preference to others. In obedience thereto I found myself in May, June, and July of this year in the Okhotsk Sea and Arctic Ocean. Both places, if not quite isolated, are still so far removed from the ordinary channels of commerce that months would elapse before any news could reach there as to the progress of termination of the American war. In consequence of this awkward circumstance I was engaged in the Arctic Ocean in acts of war as late as the 28th of June, ignorance of the serious reverses sustained by our arms in the field and the obliteration of the Government under which authority I had been acting.

This intelligence I received for the first time on communication at sea on the 2nd of August, with the British bark *Barracouta* of Liverpool, fourteen days from San Francisco. Your lordship can imagine my surprise at the receipt of such intelligence, and I would have given to it little consideration if an Englishman's opinion did not confirm the war news, though from an enemy's port.

I desisted instantly from further act of war, and determined to suspend further action until I had communication with a European port, where I would learn if that intelligence was true. It would not have been intelligent in me to convey this vessel to an American port for surrender simply because the master of the *Barracouta* had said the war was ended. I was in an embarrassing position; I diligently examined all the law writers at my command, searching a precedent for my guidance in the future control, management, and final disposal of the vessel. I could find none. History is, I believe, without a parallel.

Finding the authority questionable under which I considered this vessel a ship of war, I immediately discontinued cruising, and shaped my course for the Atlantic Ocean.

As to the ship's disposal, I do not consider that I have any right to destroy her or any further right to command her. On the contrary I think that as all the property of the Government of the United States has reverted by the fortune of war to the Government of the United States of North America, therefore this vessel, inasmuch as it was the property of the Confederate States, should accompany the other property already reverted.

I therefore sought this port as a suitable one wherein to 'learn the news' and, if I am without a government, to surrender the ship with her battery, small arms, machinery, stores, tackle and apparel complete, to Her Majesty's Government for such disposition as in its wisdom should be deemed proper.

I have, etc.

James I. Waddell

The war between the American States was finally over. It was a war that saved a great many whales, but unfortunately for the great whales of the world, the slaughter continued and after a century and a half, we still struggle to save Leviathan from the ecological insanity of our own species.

The Confederate raiders were oblivious of the real value of the work that they did. Aside from the jest by Dabney Scales, there was a complete absence of empathy for the whales nor any recognition or concern that they could be eradicated from our planet. Their focus was strictly political and economic, to do as much damage as they possibly could to Yankee commerce.

Despite this I acknowledge their contribution and I salute them for it. Every whaling ship they scuttled or burned represented lives of cetaceans saved. I am also thankful for their strategic and tactical inspiration in carrying out their destructive tasks without so much as taking the life of a single whaler.

In reading their history I was fascinated by the places they hunted and the ports and islands they found themselves. Over the last four decades, I found myself while pursuing whalers in the very same ports, operating near the very same islands and seas, unintentionally retracing the same voyages of the *Alabama*, the *Florida*, the *Shenandoah* and the other raiders.

Melbourne, Liverpool, London, Brest, Cape Town, Fernando do Noronha, Nassau, Bermuda, Gibraltar, Siberia, the Aleutians, Tahiti, Hawaii, Ascension, the South Pacific islands, the Malacca Straits, the Kerguelen Islands, the Azores, Madeira, St. Helena and so many more places, be they tropical, temperate, barren or remote.

Each and every place they ventured, I ventured, and with the pleasure of knowing their history and in many ways regarding them as fellow sailors, as if I knew and understood them.

Today the opposition to whaling is a willful opposition. There are no economic or political justifications. We defend cetaceans in the interest of cetaceans, fighting human greed and excessive destruction for the whales, not ourselves.

These magnificently noble, intelligent, social creatures continue to survive. They continue to cling to their right to swim the oceans of this planet.

Herman Melville once wrote: "Whether Leviathan can long endure so wide a chase, and so remorseless a havoc; whether he must ... like the last man, smoke his last pipe, and then himself evaporate in the final puff."

So, I work to buy them time, to cut the kill numbers by interfering with their operations, by scuttling their ships and by campaigning for their survival.

Because when that last puff of smoke that is humanity is no more, beneath that vast grey shroud of the sea, the song of the whale will prevail.

The following lists include only the whaling ships sunk during the American Civil War. The list does not include whalers that were captured and bonded nor merchant vessels other than whaling ships.

26 Whalers Sunk by the Shenandoah

Name	Type	Port	Ton		Date sunk
Edward	Bark	New Bedford	274	Burned	Dec 4, 1864
Pearl	Bark	New London		Burned	Apr 3, 1865
Hector	Ship	New Bedford		Burned	Apr 6, 1865
Edward Carey	Ship	San Francisco		Burned	Apr 6, 1865
Harvest	Bark	Honolulu		Burned	Apr 10, 1865
Abigail	Bark	New Bedford		Burned	May 27, 1865
Jireh Swift	Bark	New Bedford	428	Burned	June 22, 1865
William Thompson	Ship	New Bedford	495	Burned	June 22, 1865
Euphrates	Ship	New Bedford	364	Burned	June 22, 1865
Sophia Thornton	Ship	New Bedford	426	Burned	June 22, 1865
Nimrod	Bark	New Bedford	340	Burned	June 22, 1865
Susan Abigail	Brig	San Francisco	159	Burned	June 23, 1865
William C Nye	Bark	New Bedford	389	Burned	June 26, 1865
Catherine	Bark	New Bedford	384	Burned	June 26, 1865
Gypsey	Bark	New Bedford	360	Burned	June 26, 1865
Isabella	Bark	New Bedford	315	Burned	June 26, 1865
General Williams	Ship	New Bedford	419	Burned	June 26, 1865
Favorite	Bark	Fairhaven, MA	295	Burned	June 28, 1865
Waverly	Bark	New Bedford	327	Burned	June 28, 1865
Brunswick	Ship	New Bedford	295	Burned	June 28, 1865
Congress	Bark	New Bedford	376	Burned	June 28, 1865
Hillman	Bark	New Bedford		Burned	June 28, 1865
Isaac Howland	Ship	New Bedford	399	Burned	June 28, 1865
Nassau	Ship	New Bedford	408	Burned	June 28, 1865
Martha	Bark	New Bedford	360	Burned	June 28, 1865
Covington	Bark	New Bedford	350	Burned	June 28, 1865

1 Whaler Sunk by the Sumter

Name	Type	Port	Ton		Date sunk
Ebenezer Dodge	Bark	New Bedford	300	Burned	Dec 8, 1861

14 Whalers Sunk by the Alabama

Name	Type	Port	Ton		Date sunk
Ocmulgee	Brig	Edgartown	454	Burned	Sept 5, 1862
Starlight	Schooner	Boston	100	Burned	Sept 7, 1892
Ocean Rover	Ship	Mattapoisett	313	Burned	Sept 8, 1862
Alert	Bark	New London	398	Burned	Sept 9, 1862
Weather Gage	Schooner	Provincetown		Burned	Sept 9, 1862
Altamaha	Schooner	Sippican	119	Burned	Sept 9, 1862
Benjamin Tucker	Ship	New Bedford	349	Burned	Sept 13, 1862
Courser	Schooner	Provincetown	121	Burned	Sept 16, 1862
Virginia	Bark	New Bedford	346	Burned	Sept 17, 1862
Elisha Dunbar	Bark	New Bedford	257	Burned	Sept 18, 1862
Levi Starbuck	Ship	New Bedford	376	Burned	Nov 2, 1862
Kingfisher	Schooner	Fairhaven, MA	121	Burned	March 23, 1862
Kate Cory	Brig	Westport Point	121	Burned	April 15, 1863
Nye	Bark	New Bedford	211	Burned	Apr. 24, 1863

2 Whalers Sunk by the Florida

Name	Type	Port	Ton		Date sunk
Rienzi				Burned	July 9, 1863
Golconda			330	Burned	July 8, 1864

The Great Stone Fleet - 39 Whalers Sunk

Name	Type	Ton	Location Scuttled		Date sunk
Phoenix		404	Tybee Island, Georgia	Sunk	Dec 5, 1861
Cossack		256	Tybee Island, Georgia		Dec 8, 1861
Peter Demill	Bark	300	Tybee Island, Georgia		Dec 8, 1861

South America		606	Tybee Island, Georgia		Dec 8, 1861
Amazon	Bark	319	Morris Island, S.C.		Dec 20, 1861
America	Ship	418	Morris Island, S.C.		Dec 20, 1861
American	Bark	329	Morris Island, S.C.		Dec 20, 1861
Archer	Ship	321	Charleston, S.C.		Dec 20, 1861
Courier	Ship	381	Morris Island, S.C.		Dec 20, 1861
Fortune	Bark	310	Morris Island, S.C.		Dec 20, 1861
Garland	Ship	243	Charleston, S.C.		Dec 20, 1861
Herald	Ship	274	Morris Island, S.C.		Dec 20, 1861
Kensington	Ship	400	Charleston, S.C.		Dec 20, 1861
L.C. Richmond	Ship	383	Morris Island		Dec 20, 1861
Leonidas	Bark	320	Charleston, S.C.		Dec 20, 1861
Maria Theresa	Ship	330	Charleston, S.C.		Dec 20, 1861
Potomac	Ship	365	Charleston, S.C.		Dec 20, 1861
Rebecca Sims	Ship	400	Charleston, S.C.		Dec 20, 1861
Robin Hood	Ship	395	Charleston, S.C.		Dec 20, 1861
William Lee	Ship	311	Charleston, S.C.		Dec 20, 1861
Alvaredo	Ship		Hatteras Inlet, N.C.		Dec 20, 1861
Corea	Ship	356	Savannah, Georgia		Dec 20, 1861
Delaware Farmer	Ship		Charleston, S.C.		Dec 20, 1861
Edward	Bark	340	Un known		Dec 20, 1861
Harvest	Bark	314	Charleston, S.C.		Dec 20, 1861
Mary Francis	Ship		Charleston, S.C.		Dec 20, 1861
Montezuma	Ship	424	Charleston, S.C.		Dec 20, 1861
Meteor	Ship		Charleston, S.C.		Jan 9, 1862
Potomac			Charleston S.C.		Jan 9, 1862
Margaret Scott	Bark		Charleston, S.C.		Jan 20, 1862
Peri			Lost at Sea		Jan 24, 1862
Majestic	Ship	397	Charleston, S.C.		Jan 25, 1862
Mechanic	Ship		Charleston, S.C.		Jan 25, 1862
Messenger	Bark	216	Charleston, S.C.		Jan 25, 1862
Newburyport	Ship	341	Charleston, S.C.		Jan 25, 1862
New England	Ship	368	Charleston, S.C.		Jan 25, 1862

Noble	Bark	274	Charleston, S.C.		Jan 25, 1862
Stephen Young	Brig	200	Charleston, S.C.		Jan 25, 1862
Timor	Ship	289	Charleston, S.C.		Jan 25, 1862

Nine Ships Scuttled by Sea Shepherd

Name	Flag	Sunk	Date sunk
Sierra	Cyprus	Lisbon Harbor	February 6, 1980
Isba Uno	Spain	Vigo, Spain	April 28, 1980
Isba Dos	Spain	Vigo, Spain	April 28, 1980
Hvalur 6	Iceland	Reykjavik	November 9, 1986
Hvalur 7	Iceland	Reykjavik	November 9, 1986
Nybræna	Norway	Lofoten Islands	December 25, 1992
Senet	Norway	Gressvik	January 24, 1994
Morild	Norway	Bronnoysund	November 11, 1997
Elin-Toril	Norway	Lofoten Islands	October 31, 1997.
Willassen Senior	Norway	Svolvaer	August 30, 2007

Bibliography

Baldwin, John. Powers, Ron. Last Flag Down. The Epic Journey of the Last Confederate Warship. © 2007. Crown Publishers. New York.

Bulloch, James D. The Secret Service of the Confederate States in Europe. © 1959. Sagamore Press Inc. New York.

Chaffin, Tom. Sea of Gray. The Around the World Odyssey of the Confederate Raider Shenandoah. © 2006. Hill and Wang. New York.

Fox, Stephen. Wolf of the Deep. Raphael Semmes and the Notorious Confederate Raider CSS Alabama. © 2007 Alfred A. Knopf. New York.

Goodrich, Albert M. Cruise and Captures of the Alabama. © 1906. H.W. Wilson Co. Minneapolis.

Hearn, Chester G. Gray Raiders of the Sea. How Eight Confederate Warships Destroyed the Union's High Seas Commerce. © 1992. Louisiana State University Press.

Hunt, Cornelius E. The Shenandoah: Or, The Last Confederate Cruiser. G.W. Carleton & Co. Publishers. © 1867.

Lardas, Mark. CSS Alabama vs USS Kearsarge. Cherbourg 1864. © 2011. Osprey Publishing. Oxford, U.K.

Merli, Frank J. The Alabama. British Neutrality and the American Civil War. © 2004. Indiana University Press.

Morgan, Murray. Confederate Raider in the North Pacific. The Saga of the C.S.S. Shenandoah 1864–65. © 1995. Washington State University Press.

Schooler, Lynn. The Incredible Story of the CSS Shenandoah and the True Conclusion of the American Civil War. © 2005. Harper Collins.

Songini, Marc. The Lost Fleet – A Yankee Whaler's Struggle Against the Confederate Navy and Arctic Disaster. © 2007. St. Martha's Press. New York City.

Waddell, James I. C.S.S. Shenendoah – The Memoirs of Lieutenant Commanding James I. Waddell. Edited by James D. Horn. © 1960. Crown Publishers. (New York) 1996 published by Blue Jackets books. Naval Institute Press. Annapolis, Maryland.

California Western International Law Journal. Vol. 24 #1 Fall, 1993. The Case of the Castle John, or Greenbeard the Pirate?: Environmentalism, Piracy and the Development of International Law.

CPSIA information can be obtained
at www.ICGtesting.com
Printed in the USA
LVHW081941180619
621461LV00012B/317/P